D1550338

5.23.80

In early 1978, a group of distinguished journalists and communications experts was brought together by the Twentieth Century Fund to examine the dispute over the imbalance in the flow of information between developed and developing nations. Headed by Francoise Giroud, former French Minister of Culture, the Task Force held a series of meetings, here and abroad, listening to the views of guest witnesses and then assessing the charges and countercharges over imbalances in the flow of information and threats to freedom of the press.

The Report of the Task Force presents the conclusions and recommendations of this distinguished group, including the call for an independent body to monitor efforts designed to deal with the dispute.

A
Free
and
Balanced
Flow

A
Free
and
Balanced
Flow

Report of the
Twentieth Century Fund
Task Force on the
International Flow
of News

Background Paper
by Colin Legum
and John Cornwell

LEXINGTON BOOKS
D. C. Heath and Company
Lexington, Massachusetts
Toronto

Library of Congress Cataloging in Publication Data

Legum, Colin.
    A free and balanced flow.

    Includes bibliographical references.
    1. Foreign news.   2. Underdeveloped areas.   3. News agencies.
I. Cornwell, John, joint author.   II. Twentieth Century Fund. Task Force
on the International Flow of News.   III. Title.

PN4784.F6L4   070.4'3   78-26989
ISBN 0-87078-147-2
ISBN 0-87078-146-4 pbk.

Printed in the United States of America.

Paperbound International Standard Book Number: 0-87078-146-4

Clothbound International Standard Book Number: 0-87078-147-2

Library of Congress Catalog Card Number: 78-26989

The Twentieth Century Fund is an independent research foundation which undertakes policy studies of economic, political, and social institutions and issues. The Fund was founded in 1919 and endowed by Edward A. Filene.

CONTENTS

FOREWORD

Information is a critical commodity all over the world. As a consequence, a bitter dispute is now raging over news coverage of events in the Third World. Third World spokesmen have denounced Western newspapers, journals, and television outlets for their alleged sensationalism and anti-development bias. In reprisal, Western spokesmen have charged Third World governments with engaging in repressive acts and seeking to obstruct the free flow of information.

The governments of developing countries are clearly not hostile to information as such; on the contrary, they are well aware of its value in speeding material development and in maintaining power. But many governments seek to control the content of news about their activities and the dissemination of news from abroad to their own citizens and particularly to their opposition. The desire for such control motivates the demands for a "new information order," which the news organizations of the West regard as a threat to the freedom to report, to print, and to broadcast news.

Given its continuing interest in domestic and foreign communications issues, the Twentieth Century Fund has closely followed the exchange of charges and countercharges between those demanding balance in the news and those demanding journalistic freedom. A year ago, the Fund's Board of Trustees decided to bring together representatives of the two sides to explore the issues underlying the dispute and to attempt to resolve it. It chose to convene an independent, international Task Force made up of authorities on communications from both the developed and the developing countries.

The Task Force was ably and deftly chaired by Francoise Giroud of

ix

France. Its members had diverse backgrounds and interests, but they shared a sense that prolongation of the dispute served no one's interests. They sought to make a positive contribution and exhibited a willingness to work long and hard to achieve it. They also chose to hear from a number of guests with considered positions. These guests included Sean MacBride, chairman of UNESCO's International Communications Commission; Dr. Hernan Santa Cruz, president of the Center for International Development; Altaf Gauhar of Third World Media; Edward Ploman, director of the International Broadcast Institute; and Henry Raymont of the Organization of American States; they made statements and then answered the Task Force's questions. The Task Force and the Fund are indebted to them.

In its deliberations, the Task Force sought to distinguish between the justified grievances and the inflamed rhetoric of some Third World critics. The result of these deliberations appears in the Task Force Report, a well reasoned and perceptive analysis of the serious imbalance in the flow of news, and the difficulty of righting it. The Report further contributes to the debate by demonstrating that a free flow of news is as important to the developing world as it is—and has been—to the West. And the recommendations of the Task Force point the way to ending the conflict that has proved so divisive and counterproductive.

The Fund is grateful to the entire Task Force and especially to Mme. Giroud, who enabled each member to express his views freely and fully, while keeping the discussion sharply focused on the critical issues. Hers was a demanding assignment, and she carried it out superbly. I also want to express thanks to Colin Legum and John Cornwell, who collaborated on the background paper that accompanies the Report of the Task Force; Legum served as a member of the Task Force and Cornwell as its rapporteur.

M. J. Rossant, DIRECTOR
The Twentieth Century Fund
November 1978

Task Force Members

Francoise Giroud, chairman,
formerly editor, L'Express;
formerly minister of culture,
Paris

Elie Abel,
dean, School of Journalism,
Columbia University

Harry J. Boyle,
retiring chairman, Canadian Radio and
Telecommunications Commission,
Toronto

Abdelkader Chanderli
formerly Algerian Representative
to the United States and
the United Nations, Geneva

Alberto Dines,
political columnist, Folha
de São Paulo, *Rio de Janiero*

Henry Grunwald,
corporate editor, Time, Inc.,
New York

Thilo Koch,
television writer,
Wurtenberg, Germany

Colin Legum,
associate editor, The Observer,
London

Flora Lewis,
chief European correspondent,
The New York Times, *Paris*

Georges-Henri Martin,
editor-in-chief, La Tribune
de Geneve, *Geneva*

Carlos Monsivais,
television journalist;
anthropologist, Mexico City

S. Nihal Singh,
editor, The Statesman, Ltd.,
Calcutta

Frank Stanton,
formerly president, Columbia
Broadcasting System, New York

Roger Tatarian,
formerly vice-president, UPI;
professor of journalism, California
State University

David Webster,
director, public affairs,
British Broadcasting Corporation,
London

Benjamin Whitaker,
writer; director, Minority
Rights Group, London

John Cornwell, rapporteur,
editor, Observer News Service,
London

Report of the Task Force

Even though the post-World War II movement toward political independence in the developing world has been largely accomplished, the developing nations of Africa, Asia, and Latin America still maintain that they are being victimized in their relations with the advanced industrial countries. The Third World has been calling for a new economic order on the ground that the West has persisted in its domination of international trade and finance. It is now calling for a new world information order as well, accusing Western news agencies and press, both print and electronic, of providing a flow of news that is unbalanced, distorted, and ethnocentric.

This antagonism in the Third World has its roots in the age of imperialism, when the West's military and economic hegemony was accompanied by a supremacy in communications. By implanting its institutions in foreign soil and by imposing its attitudes, more or less by fiat, the West constricted the Third World's cultural self-identity, thereby causing independent developing nations to become even more hostile and aggressive.

The demand for a new information order has provoked a particularly bitter dispute. Spokesmen for a number of Third World governments are currently seeking to establish regional and international news agencies under state auspices in order to achieve a greater balance in the flow of news. They advocate the promotion of "developmental" journalism as a means of fostering their own values and objectives and at the same time correcting distortions and eliminating what they claim is a Western predilection for crises, scandals, and trivialities. For their part, representatives of Western communications enterprises have charged that these Third World demands for governmental involvement threaten press freedom and the dissemination of news around the world.

Against this background of charge and countercharge, the Twentieth Century Fund established an independent, international Task Force that it hoped would go beyond the inflammatory rhetoric of both sides

3

to explore practical means of resolving the conflict. The Task Force on the International Flow of News brought together journalists, commentators, and editors from both the West and the Third World, all of whom participated as private individuals rather than as representatives of their organizations or countries. It might well have been expected that such a diverse group would be unable to agree on either the dimensions of the problem or its resolution. But in the course of its deliberations, the Task Force found itself agreeing—to a remarkable extent—on both basic principles and practical proposals.

The Task Force believes that there is a serious imbalance in the flow of information between the developing and the developed nations. It believes that this imbalance can be reduced by improving the quality of information and also by increasing the quantity of Third World news appearing in Western print or electronic outlets. It goes without saying that such an improvement depends in large part on fuller and better coverage of developments in the Third World, which in turn involves greater access for Western journalists; it also depends on better coverage by the Third World's communications outlets of local and regional developments as well as of news from the West.

Some Third World governments have persuaded themselves that the best way to eliminate the imbalance is for them to gain control of the flow of information. The desire of politicians to control broadcasting and the press is, of course, as much a staple of the developed as of the developing world. Governments in both the West and the Third World, in fact, have again and again both denied access to journalists and sought to control the shape and content of domestic and foreign news. This Task Force believes that such efforts are ultimately self-defeating. The imposition of either formal or informal controls over communications will not only hinder the flow of information but also have deleterious effects on the quantity and quality of information disseminated in the West and in the Third World.

No amount of economic or political pressure exerted by the Third World can force the free press in developed countries to print what it does not wish to print. This Task Force urgently suggests, therefore, that the Third World encourage cooperation between print and electronic media in both developing and developed countries in the interests of improving access to technical and communications facilities.

The Task Force acknowledges that news about Third World events receives relatively little coverage in either the developed or the developing countries but rejects the notion that this imbalance is the result of either a political or an economic conspiracy on the part of Western interests. Rather, it sees the imbalance as the inevitable consequence of historical and technological developments, owing particularly to the spread of colonialism.

Also, if Western news agencies predominate in servicing the press around the world and if Western radio and television corporations predominate in transmitting news, information, and entertainment, it is for the simple reason that most news originates in the West and concerns Western events. Much of the imbalance is also the result of the strong tendency of all regions, nations, and races toward ethnocentricity. (Polls, for example, have shown that there is little interest among Third World countries in news about other Third World countries.)

The distortions that occur in Western reporting are rarely deliberate; most are the result of cultural differences. Thus, improvement in the balance of information presupposes a commitment on the part of the press in the developed nations—especially of the "gatekeepers," the editors and producers, of the print and broadcasting organizations—to become more familiar with the culture and conditions in developing countries.

Above all, what is called for is a greater accuracy and a qualitative improvement in the selection, writing, and presentation of material. But accuracy cannot be attained unless journalists are allowed the freedom to move and to report; and better selection of material, giving a needed sense of balance, requires gatekeepers who are sensitive and informed about the diverse interests of the world community.

The Task Force is not under the illusion that the situation is amenable to quick or easy remedial action. It is convinced that some of the proposals put forward by representatives of Third World governments would be detrimental to the objective of a more equitable balance in the flow of news. For example, "a new information order," predicated on an already existing order in communications, might well further impede the flow of information around the world. Similarly, demands for greater government participation are likely to result in increasing confrontation rather than cooperation between the West and the Third World. Given the technological advantages now possessed by Western print and electronic news organizations, Third World attempts to redress the imbalance by government intervention or control can only perpetuate inequality in the flow of news.

The Task Force concludes that the problem can best be handled by self-critical and cooperative efforts based on mutual self-interest. **It is our unanimous and deeply held belief that freedom of information and economic and political development are inextricably intertwined and mutually reinforcing.**

We recognize that it is impossible to decree freedom of information; such freedom must be worked for. Because freedom of the press is fragile, even in the West, where reliance on government sources has often been excessive and where informal pressures have sometimes been successful, it is unrealistic to expect that it will be embraced everywhere. Unstable or authoritarian regimes will never be willing to countenance a free flow of information. Yet the history of the West demonstrates that freedom of information has been an integral part of economic and political development, and the experience of India, where suppression of press freedom proved politically disastrous, is a shining demonstration from the Third World.

While the Task Force believes in a free flow of information, it also favors a more balanced flow of information, but these are two very different concepts.

A free flow of information, in its simplest form, is the freedom or right of journalists to travel, ask questions, and transmit their reports. A balanced flow of information is the provision of ample coverage and the transmission of news events to and about the world community.

Freedom of information tends to flourish where pluralistic ownership of news outlets creates checks and balances that assure a high degree of competition and accountability. But more is involved than pluralistic ownership of a variety of publications, radio stations, and television channels or a multiplicity of sources of information; there also must be a plurality of opinions, freely held and freely expressed. This kind of freedom has been most in evidence in the West, where democratic institutions are well established and where there is no direct government interference or control over printed or broadcast information. The essence of a free flow of information, as it is perceived in the West, is that it should serve the public—readers, listeners, and viewers—not the government.

Authoritarian regimes, on the other hand, insist on controlling information on the ground that the interests of their citizens are synonymous with the interests of the state. Such regimes achieve control easily, moving from state monopoly ownership to actual censorship (formal and informal) of the information made available to the public and often even to prohibition of the sale of foreign newspapers and journals.

Frequently, when contriving to keep information about internal developments from foreign journalists, authoritarian regimes resort to such measures as barring entry, restricting travel, denying access to government sources, and threatening expulsion or even imprisonment. The Third World is not a monolith: some developing countries have authoritarian regimes that exercise rigid control over the press; a few are willing to tolerate a large measure of press freedom.

But most countries of the Third World are pursuing a middle course. Because they take the position that economic and social conditions do not yet permit a free flow of information, they believe that their communications systems should be partly or, in some cases, extensively controlled by the state. Still, they hold out the hope that this kind of control will one day be relaxed. Some developing countries have already taken commendable steps in that direction—for example, by allowing comment critical of the government to appear in their newspapers and in many cases by giving foreign journalists access to sources of information.

In democratic, pluralistic countries, wire agencies or broadcasting companies sponsored or owned by the state can still enjoy a large measure of freedom in the coverage and transmission of information. Such quasi-governmental organizations as Agence France Press and such public authorities as the British Broadcasting Corporation have probably helped to disperse control and have thus contributed to the free flow of information, whereas those state-sponsored or state-owned news organizations that are subject to control in terms of the information they disseminate cannot be described as providing either a free or a balanced flow of information.

Nevertheless, many developing nations argue that the present imbalance in the flow of information can be at least partially redressed by state intervention. The Task Force maintains, however, that a state can be the arbiter neither of what constitutes a balanced flow of information in regard to its own policies nor of what is and is not balanced in the international flow of news; apart from anything else, state-controlled news is almost by definition suspect as propaganda. If any progress toward better balance is to be made, one thing is certain: it will not come through governmental intervention or control.

The Task Force believes that there is a broad enough area of common ground between many countries of the Third World and the countries of the West to move forward in a cooperative search for new measures to improve the balance in the international flow of news. We do not believe that progress toward this objective can be made by taking punitive action against the major press agencies of the West. These agencies have begun to respond constructively to criticisms of imbalance and ethnocentricity; they have taken steps to effectively "decolonize" their operations by substantially increasing employment and training opportunities for representatives of Third World countries and by greatly expanding their coverage and transmission of news about these countries.

To be sure, attempts to produce a better balance in the flow of news remain inadequate. But the flow of news is not merely a function of a more equitable distribution of manpower and technology. One reason that more news—political, economic, and social—about the West is carried by the wire services is that the West is a great power center, made up of the most advanced and powerful nations in the world; its news is therefore of international significance.

As developing countries become stronger economically, they will inevitably generate more news. In the meantime, fresh efforts are needed to promote better coverage of development by the great international news agencies—the wholesalers of news—and by the print and electronic press—the retailers of news—thereby informing the general public in the West and in the Third World about the benefits that can result from a freer flow of news.

Many Third World spokesmen have made Western news agencies the scapegoat for the failure of newspapers and broadcasters in both the advanced and the developing nations to provide more information about Third World events. This criticism is unfair. The agencies transmit daily a substantial amount of news about the Third World, but most of their copy is neither printed nor broadcast. Limitations of space and time obviously restrict the number of news agency stories that can be used by news retailers, each of which sets its own criteria for what it makes available to readers or viewers. In the West, for example, the standards for selection used by the popular press are very different from those used by the quality press. The charge that must be answered is that even the quality press, which is of particular concern to the leaders of the Third World, does not publish enough about the developing countries and that a good deal of what it does publish fails to reflect economic and political realities.

As always, the first step in solving a problem is to acknowledge its existence. Despite the Task Force's disagreement with those proposing a new international order in communications, it recognizes that they have made a significant contribution emphasizing the imbalance in the international flow of news. As a consequence, the major purveyors of information have become increasingly sensitive to the demands and needs of the Third World. Further progress depends on promoting among news retailers and the public in the West an awareness of the need for a balanced flow of information and on engendering among the developing countries a greater appreciation of the value of a free flow of information. The Task Force hopes that the proposals and recommendations that follow will serve both these objectives.

The Task Force recommends the establishment of a private body composed of independent journalists and specialists in communications from both the developed and the developing countries, to monitor, evaluate, and report suggestions and proposals for dealing with a free and more balanced flow of information. One of the primary purposes of such a body would be to maintain the principle of "pluralism" by counterbalancing and scrutinizing initiatives set by governmental, intergovernmental, or quasi-governmental institutions. By issuing regular appraisals of new suggestions, the proposed body could stimulate more informed and more thorough debate.

The Task Force believes that no institution, however useful it may be, presently performs this essential task. Some organizations are devoted to the problems of the print press, others to those of broadcasting; still others are made up solely of either Western or Third World representatives or are under governmental auspices. The Task Force's proposal calls for a body of independent professionals who would be responsible for appraising the problems of print and electronic journalism in order to make progress toward a free—and more balanced—flow of information. Such a body would certainly benefit from the knowledge and experience of other institutions, but it must be completely free to exercise its own judgments.

In order to emphasize that the assignment of this independent body is both temporary and discrete, devoted solely to helping resolve the current dispute, we propose that it be called the Ad Hoc Committee for the International Flow of News. We further propose that it be in operation for no more than two years, which we believe is ample time to assess the work of UNESCO's International Communications Commission as well as the reports of similar bodies.

Various members of the Task Force made other recommendations, among them the establishment of an international agency to handle requests and inquiries about the many financial and training opportunities available to journalists. Such an agency would coordinate programs sponsored by nongovernmental bodies, regional organizations, universities, and schools of journalism. The programs, aimed at improving the flow of information in developing countries, would provide technical assistance for the press, news agencies, broadcasting, television, and technical communications systems and would give journalists, broadcasters, and others professionally involved in the communications systems of developing nations—especially in foreign reporting—the opportunity both to utilize their skills and to learn new ones.

Another proposal strongly endorsed by some members of the Task Force was for the establishment of an international press fund to award grants to experienced journalists working for newspapers or broadcasting companies in both Western and developing countries, enabling them to investigate and report international news. In recent years, the number of foreign correspondents from the Western media has dwindled, partly because of the prohibitively high costs entailed in supporting staff in foreign posts. High costs also inhibit Third World press and broadcasters from maintaining more than a handful of foreign correspondents.

The fund, which would be administered by a private board of trustees, would make grants in consultation with the recipients' newspapers, perhaps on a sabbatical pay or a partial financing basis. But management of cooperating papers or broadcast outlets would not be relieved of the responsibility for assigning journalists and apportioning budgets. In some cases, funds might be specifically allocated to defray the costs of transmission, film crews, or studios. The fund also might help subsidize the efforts of independent writers and journalists working on projects that could be the fodder for a worthy book or film about developing countries.

The Task Force also endorses a proposal that was presented to the 1978 Cairo Conference on the International Media and the Developing World for the establishment of a Multinational News Agency (MNA) that would be supported by news agencies of both developed and developing countries.* The MNA would have a central directorate of approximately twelve members, half from Western and half from developing countries. Members of the existing Nonaligned News Pool would make up half of the directorate of the MNA, and the other half would be drawn from press organizations represented by the World Free Press Development Committee.

An equal number of news agencies and newspapers on each side would be asked to lend the MNA the services of an experienced reporter for a period of no less than one year. Although the salaries of these reporters would be paid by their regular employers, the reporters would be assigned to countries other than their own by the multinational pool; the Task Force believes that this measure would help produce more news of international import.

The reportage of these special MNA correspondents would be made available for general distribution simultaneously to all participating agencies. The MNA would not compete with or otherwise affect the operations of any existing agency. In fact, its operation would be sustained by the large international and regional agencies, such as the Nonaligned Pool or the projected Pan-African News Agency.

Funds for the expenses of the special reports and for a central editing operation of the MNA would be raised by members of the directorate from both public and private sources. In order to prevent domination by either side, agreed-on limits would be placed on governmental contributions.

Once established, the directorate of the MNA could serve as a central clearinghouse or bridge to other forms of cooperation among journalists of the two worlds.

These proposals, along with the accompanying list put forward during our deliberations by various other groups concerned about the impediments to a freer flow and better balance of news, require thorough and independent scrutiny. The Task Force believes that the new inde-

---

*See Roger Tatarian, "The Multinational News Pool," paper for the Edward R. Murrow Center of Public Diplomacy Conference on "The International News Media and the Developing World," April 2–5, 1978, Cairo.

pendent and ad hoc committee that it suggests establishing—a body that would be supported by foundations and other private sources and whose members would be experts in the field of communications from both the West and the developing countries—is ideally suited to perform this function. Such a body can fill a critical gap by providing informed and disinterested analysis that no organization is at present equipped to fill.

The Task Force believes that this proposed monitoring and evaluating board has a still more significant role to play in stimulating public interest in and concern about the current imbalance in the flow of news and the dangers posed by governmental attempts to control or limit the free flow of information. In the face of ethnocentric pressures, the insecurity—and suspicions—of governments, and the economic and technological advantages of the West, no single group can solve the problem by itself. But such a board can create a greater public awareness of the important issues involved. Conversely, it can point out what not to do and thus help avoid a papering over or minimizing of the problem. Cooperation and compromise are obviously necessary when working toward a free flow and a better balance of news, but the Task Force is unanimous in its belief that there can be no compromise over basic principles.

We trust that if the new board is established it will defend freedom of the press where it exists, help to develop freedom where it does not, and strengthen its position in the development process.

We reject out of hand the view that freedom is something that only the developed nations of the West can afford—and that it is a superfluous luxury for the developing nations. The practices of a free press may be erratic, even in the West, but the aspirations of freedom should ultimately serve to unite the West and the Third World.

PLEA FOR MORE DEVELOPMENT NEWS
by Georges-Henri Martin

In addition to the proposals and statements of principle formulated by the Task Force, I would suggest the following:

1. The organization of seminars for the "gatekeepers" in television, radio, or newspapers, in order to stimulate the interest of editors and producers in developmental news.

2. The organization of hearings in national legislatures in developed nations or in the parliamentary committees or congressional committees on technical assistance and development, in order to make the public aware of the problems and prospects of the Third World. For the same purpose, the organization of government-sponsored programs of school lectures or "youth forums" with international officials or representatives of developing nations as speakers.

3. As recommended in the January 1978 issue of *The Columbia Journalism Review*, major newspapers, magazines, wire services, and television networks could send experienced reporters to live in villages in Asia, Africa, and Latin America for a period of between four and six months, each accompanied by a full-time, locally hired interpreter, and to report the findings in feature stories with photographs. I recommend that such an effort be coordinated with the 1979 meeting of the World Conference on Agrarian Reform and Rural Development in Rome. This conference would give the mass media an opportunity to report on the daily life of the world's peasantry, who have been the point of departure for all the great contemporary revolutions.

4. I support the suggestion of Ambassador Abdelkader Chanderli that, whenever a project for technical cooperation is drawn up within the agencies of the United Nations, a budget should be set aside to finance information for those interested.

5. The information produced by the United Nations on development tends to stay in a "ghetto" consisting of UN and nongovernmental experts who are sealed away from the public. I propose that a newsletter, modeled on the one developed by the Boy Scouts World Bureau, be created to report on the north-south dialogue and aimed at gatekeepers, parliamentarians, and policymakers. The north-south dialogue might be facilitated by using electronics less and air-mail communications more. And the mass media might make a greater effort to link international activities to local situations—for example, by showing that the UNCTAD Conference on cocoa affected the lives of both the small planter in the Third World and the American schoolboy drinking his cup of hot chocolate.

Paraphrasing the late Lester Markel, I feel that development news is not foreign news, that it is real "local" news. To facilitate the north-south understanding, UN publications intended for the general public could be made available to travelers on trains and airlines.

6. Within professional organizations of journalists, special commit-tees could be set up to monitor progress in the north-south dialogue and possibly to produce an annual survey of communications prob-lems.

7. Editorial pages in Western dailies could be more widely opened to guest contributors from Third World countries.

8. A greater effort could certainly be made to cooperate with the various "institutes of communications" attached to all major universi-ties in Third World countries, and particularly in both English- and French-speaking Africa.

The Task Force is clearly motivated by a desire to develop a better dialogue with the mass media of the "gray areas"—those countries that do not enjoy complete freedom of the press but that, on the other hand, do not suffer the censorship of totalitarian regimes. In these gray areas, the teaching staffs of the institutes of communications have a practical knowledge of the steps that must be taken before local press freedom and better north-south dialogue can be achieved. In my view, the Twentieth Century Fund's Task Force should encourage coopera-tion with the countries belonging to the gray areas of partial press free-dom in the hope of moving them toward greater freedom.

Background Paper
by Colin Legum and John Cornwell

A CRITICAL DEBATE

It is surprising how many people . . . hardly know of the existence of this debate [about the free flow of information], and of its present critical stage. When they do learn of it, they are usually inclined to argue at first that nothing can be done to improve matters, to imply that international market mechanisms have the force of acts of God or to bring out the routine assertions about the principle of free circulation, as though the consequences of the interplay between that principle and market mechanisms are not even to be examined.

This is not good enough. More can be done than we are usually disposed to think, and should be done. Not just because to continue shrugging off the very existence of a problem plays straight into the hands of the dictators in some developing countries, and it is their own people who then suffer even greater deprivation; nor just because our laissez-faire stance seems to confirm what the Soviet Union tells the developing countries about the real intentions of the West; nor just because unless we do show more understanding, regressive measures will be taken by developing countries to cut back the import of Western material, and we may not be happy with what goes and what stays. We have to do more, above all, because not to do so is lazy and selfish to an inexcusable degree.

—Dr. Richard Hoggart
Assistant Director-General
of UNESCO, 1970–75

I/The Roots of the Controversy

"And nations shall speak unto nations. . . ."

It is a fact that the world's communications system is dominated by Western institutions. The reasons for this imbalance are partly historic (at one time much of the Third World was under the control of Western nations) and partly inevitable (those with greater power tend to exercise greater influence).

Today, both the Third World* and the Communist world are attempting to redress the balance in the flow of information. And the stronger the Third World grows, the greater will be its ability to achieve essential changes in the international communications system.

But it is not enough to say that the Third World must wait patiently until it is strong enough to compel change. Serious attempts should be made now to ameliorate the situation without waiting for the balance in world power to change.

A determined effort to help redress the balance in the flow of information is as important to champions of freedom of the press as it is to the Third World. The present system is unjust, and those who are concerned with freedom must be equally concerned with justice; it should therefore

* *A note on nomenclature:* In this study, the terms "Third World," "the south," and "developing nations" are used interchangeably to refer to those mostly newly independent nations of Africa, Asia, Latin America, the Middle East, and the Caribbean and Pacific areas, which have chosen to identify themselves neither with the First World (the West) nor with the Second World (the Soviet bloc). Most, although not all, of these belong to the grouping of nonaligned nations that operates as a powerful force within the international system. All are members of the "Group of 77," the core of the association of developing nations that operates as a pressure group against the industrialized nations (Western and Communist) within the framework of the United Nations Conference on Trade and Development (UNCTAD).

fall to them to provide leadership in helping to reduce manifest inequities. Moreover, we can no longer afford to ignore the fact that the present imbalance in the flow of information is a serious impediment to international harmony and cooperation. If only for reasons of pure self-interest, the Western countries must take into account what they stand to lose by alienating Third World nations, especially those that share our democratic aspirations. Also, there are very real dangers to the international community when it is not accurately informed about developments in Third World countries.

Although the potential confrontation posed by the Third World is different from that posed by the Soviet bloc, the Communist nations have involved themselves in the international controversy about the free flow of news. Soviet intervention has served to further cloud the issues in the dispute between the Third World and the West—making it even more difficult to assess the validity of the structural changes in the international communications system being demanded by the Third World and to examine critically the international news coverage of the Western mass media. And the extreme attitudes adopted by a number of anti-Western critics in the Third World have tended to produce a defensiveness on the part of certain Western spokesmen who seek to present the controversy largely in terms of a struggle for "the defense of press freedom" against an authoritarian challenge.

Before rushing to man the barricades in defense of "press freedom," however, we must examine whether it is in fact possible to achieve a free flow of information within the present international communications system, and whether the Western mass media have indeed been above reproach in their handling of sensitive international issues.

Two assumptions are made in this study: first, the Third World has established a *prima facie* case for its claims that structural reforms of the international communications system are necessary if nations are "to talk to nations" and that these claims require careful study and understanding; second, freedom of information can most efficiently be promoted through a free press with a minimum of constraints imposed by governments or their agencies. The ideological "slant" of this analysis is therefore against those who argue that structural reforms of the international communications system require—indeed, demand—greater state control, which has been the major element introduced into this controversy by the Communist world, by Western Marxists, and by some non-Marxist spokesmen in the Third World.

What the Controversy Is About

It is not a coincidence that freedom of information and human rights have become issues of world concern at approximately the same time— for the freedom to know and to communicate constitutes a vital human right; without this freedom, other human rights cannot be pursued effectively either within national borders or within the world community.

The expansion of human rights therefore depends largely on the success of expanding the free flow of information *within the borders of individual nations, as well as between and among nations.*

What exactly is meant when we talk about improving the "free flow of information"? The current controversy shows a strong tendency to equate "free flow" with a "balanced flow." Yet these are not necessarily the same; they may, in fact, be incompatible.

Many of the proposals to secure a better "balance" in the flow of information seek, instead, to curb a "free flow." One argument frequently advanced is that "balance" can be obtained only by interfering with the way in which news is collected, distributed, and presented; hence, the argument in favor of more government control over the sources and distribution of information.

Those who have stubbornly resisted restraints on news gathering, distribution, and presentation in their own countries, in the name of the long struggle to defend and expand press freedom, can hardly be expected to submit to government controls on the international level.

Just how is "balance" to be determined, and by whom? Almost all governments sooner or later arrive at the conclusion that their policies are not presented in a balanced or fair way by the media; many governments feel particularly aggrieved by the ways in which their policies or aspirations are reflected abroad—and the more tyrannical, corrupt, or inefficient they are, the more strongly they feel.

It is manifestly unacceptable that governments should be the arbiters of how their own policies should be presented. But this is precisely what would occur if it were agreed that, for the sake of "balance," a greater degree of government control should be imposed over the sources of news or over the channels through which news is distributed.

Governments undoubtedly have a role to play in the organization and, especially, in the distribution of news. Most broadcasting and television corporations in the world, including those in Western countries, are state-controlled, while some of the international news agencies are either subsidized or indirectly controlled by the state. Yet it is one thing to acknowledge that governments might justifiably have a role to play in the conduct of the mass media, and quite another to claim that they should have the right to dominate not only their own mass media (as is the case in authoritarian societies) but foreign media as well.

To yield on any of the essential principles governing a free press in order to achieve a "balance" in the flow of international news would vitiate the principles of a "free flow." It is therefore necessary that we distinguish between a "balanced flow" and a "free flow" of news.

Another confusion in the debate concerns both the "quantity" and "quality" of news flowing through the news-gathering agencies. It would be a relatively simple matter to increase the quantity of information reaching the news desks of the media, but this guarantees neither an increase in the quantity of information between the Third World and Western audiences nor an improvement in the quality of that information.

The central issue in the debate is the *quality* of the information going onto the wires or into print or across the radio or onto the television screen. The concern is not only with accurately informing Western audiences about developing societies but, equally, with ensuring that Third World audiences receive a full and balanced picture of the West, not just, as happens too frequently, of the fripperies and trivia that are invariably the by-products of affluent societies. To this end, the "gate-keepers" of both the Western and the Third World media must have a greater understanding about the impact of their societies on one another.

The maximum effort should go into improving the quality of information. Indeed, this should be established as the primary objective. The result will be a welcome decrease in the amount of traffic passing through information channels.

The term "quality" also needs to be defined, if only broadly. It is something more than a striving for the impossible ideal of "objectivity." A "fair balance" can be ensured only by combining "positive" and "negative" reporting; both are inevitable, and both are necessary. What is unfair is that often the emphasis in the information appearing about certain Third World countries is adverse, while that appearing about other countries is favorable, owing perhaps to their oil wealth or their strategic importance. There will always be a place for straight information, but there also is a need for critical reporting and analysis. And "copy" should ideally be both interesting and well written. The proper concern is therefore with *standards* of journalism, in both the Western and the Third World media.

Some governments favor extending control over their national media into the international field because they believe that their development policies are inadequately—and at times even incorrectly—reported. This is an argument frequently summoned up by Third World governments to criticize their own media—as was the case in India during Indira Gandhi's administration. Those who use these arguments—often from the best motives—fail to understand that information disseminated through a controlled media is ipso facto treated with suspicion both at home and abroad.

A basic misconception exists about the value of government-controlled information in promoting greater knowledge about development. Indeed, few would believe what they read if they knew that it had been vetted by the governments of the countries concerned.

That the present system governing the flow of information, within and among nations, is in many respects inadequate is a given in this debate. No country can fairly claim to have a completely free system of mass communication, but only authoritarian societies contrive to impede the development of a free press.

The current controversy has thrown into sharp focus the different "world views" of the role of the mass media in society. On one side are those who take the liberal democratic view that the essence of a free press is that it should be pluralist both in its ownership and in the interests it serves and that, above all, it should be immune to direct government intervention and control. On the other side is the authoritarian view that insists that state ownership and, hence, control over the mass media are indispensable to a press run in the best interests of its readers.

The different approaches inevitably polarize discussion on how the present inadequate flow of news might best be improved. But between these two opposites there exists a third view held by those who favor, or in any case accept, the notion that the mass media should be partly free and partly controlled as instruments of state policy.

The Third World governments remain largely unpersuaded by the arguments of either the liberal democrats or the authoritarians. But even within the third grouping, there are governments, media people, and others concerned with the political process who generally favor one view over the other.

The current debate is concerned with how best to improve the present system. One approach holds that the international system of communications can be improved only, or mainly, by increasing the degree of government control over the mass media, for example, over news agencies and over the role of communicators; the other approach holds that increasing government controls will seriously damage the flow of "free" news. These two attitudes are of course irreconcilable.

It must be admitted that the flow of news—particularly between the Western nations and the Third World—is heavily imbalanced in favor of the West. It is not, therefore, surprising that Third World leaders and intellectuals—including those who share aspirations for a free press—should think that their societies are at a serious disadvantage.

The industrialized nations must improve their knowledge of the culture and needs of developing countries. Much of the distortion in the reporting of news concerning Third World nations is due to ignorance. The balance in the news transmitted is sure to be greatly improved once the Western media improve their understanding of—as well as their attitude toward—Third World countries. This requires a greater degree of specialization from those engaged in reporting from developing countries.

However, those engaged in foreign reporting are not the only ones who should be better informed; the "gatekeepers," those who control editorial policies and who determine what is published, also must strive for a greater understanding of the problems of the developing world—if only to be able to relate them to the problems of their own countries.

In the media as elsewhere, learning is a two-way process. It is not enough for Western communicators to help Third World communicators to do their job better; Western communicators must share in the experience of learning.

Communication too is, and by definition, a two-way process, not only in its more technical aspects of gathering and conveying news, but also in understanding the essential mutual interests shared by different parts of international society.

While the dichotomy between those who believe in the virtues of an "open society" and those who defend the ideologies of a "closed society" is clear-cut, it is a great mistake to approach the Third World as if it were locked into the ideas of authoritarian systems or as if it were a bloc of homogeneous nations. Despite military regimes, single-party states, and other semiauthoritarian political systems, a great part of the Third World aspires to freedom in its fullest sense. The strength of these aspirations should be recognized, not dismissed out of hand because of the nature of a particular regime. In the case of the newest nations in the Third World, most regimes turn out to be transitory.

Great differences exist within the Third World—both in the levels of development and in the establishment of pluralistic institutions (including the press). It should be possible to achieve quick results with programs of cooperation aimed at those societies that already have gone some way toward acquiring a sophisticated habit of democratic practice.

The governments and intellectuals of such countries also offer opportunities for establishing a strong alliance in the debate over how best to promote a freer and better balanced flow of information.

An alliance between those in the West and those in the Third World who believe in the value of a free press could play a decisive role in expanding freedom within the Third World and in improving standards of international reporting in the Western press. By working together to help overcome the major obstacles to the free flow of information, both sides could contribute to reducing some of the causes of hostility and misunderstanding that characterize so much of the relations between the Third World and the Western nations.

A Historical Perspective

The controversy over the international flow of news has developed alongside another north-south controversy: the demand for a New International Economic Order (NIEO). The connection between the two is not accidental: both are intrinsic to the growing confrontation between the Third World and the West and, as such, constitute a vital aspect of contemporary history. The significance of this confrontation can be understood only by grasping the extent of the revolutionary changes that have been eroding the international system for the last thirty years.

The end of World War II marked the beginning of what might be described as the postimperial era. It is one of those watersheds in history when the balance of power shifts decisively, when new forces and ideas take shape—as in the Renaissance, the Hundred Years War, and the Industrial Revolution. The generations who lived through those important periods had been unable to see the separate episodes as belonging to a single historic process of change, but we see the interrelationship of four great changes that have been occurring in our lifetime and that are bringing about a radically different international system.

The first of these changes has been the erosion of Western dominance in international affairs. Before World War II, the ability of the Western nations, individually or in alliances, to impose their will on the non-Western world was incontestable. The great power struggles of the European imperial era were all fought among the Western nations themselves. The Industrial Revolution had given the West a headstart over the rest of the world in creating new wealth and accumulating great military power, which in turn resulted both in the expansion of European imperialism and in the rise of the United States. However, the technological advances of the Industrial Revolution did not remain an exclusively Western possession, and we are now witnessing the recession of the power of the West.

The second major change has been the rise of the Soviet Union (not international communism) as one of the two superpowers.

The third significant change has been the emergence of China as a potential world power. Although in military terms not yet a challenge to the two superpowers, China has begun to mobilize her economic potential, and her influence has begun to spread to most areas of the world.

The fourth great change has been the emergence of the Third World as a major factor in world affairs. Mostly former colonial dependencies,

the nations of the Third World are by no means a cohesive force; nor are
they likely to become so, except when their independence or their ability
to engage in world trade is threatened. Thus, the concept of NIEO
represents an important shared aspiration of the developing nations,
while the movement of nonaligned nations is an expression of their
aspiration toward independence from either of the major military power
blocs.

The NIEO represents the aspirations of the developing nations to
restructure the entire international system of trade and finance, which
has for centuries been dominated by the industrialized nations, mainly
of the West and Japan. The charter of the NIEO was adopted at the
fourth Nonaligned Summit Conference in Algiers in September 1973[1]
and was formally approved at the special session of the UN General
Assembly in May 1974.

At the same time, the Algiers conference recognized that an integral
aspect of the Third World's demand for the transformation of the
international economic system required that it ''take concerted action in
the field of mass communication . . . in order to promote a greater
interchange of ideas among themselves.''

Although UNESCO had begun to investigate problems of the free
flow of information as early as 1952 (see The Role of UNESCO, below),
it was at the Algiers meeting that the issue first surfaced as one of major
international concern. Initially, though, the thrust of the resolutions
adopted at Algiers was toward achieving a freer flow of information
among the nonaligned countries. One of the resolutions called on
members to ''exchange and disseminate information concerning their
mutual achievements in all fields'' through their own news media; this
seeded the idea that the nonaligned nations should form their own news
''pool.''

In its original concept, therefore, the ''pool'' was not conceived of as
a rival to, let alone as a supplanter of, the major Western news agencies.
It was only later—when the challenge over the proposed NIEO developed into an open north-south confrontation and when UNESCO's
studies began to concentrate on the importance of a two-way flow of
information between the developed and the developing nations—that
the Third World challenge came to be felt as a ''threat'' both to the
Western press traditions and to a freer flow of information.

After 1974, Third World leaders, trying to evoke an urgent and
positive response from Western leaders and the public to their call for a
NIEO, experienced three overwhelmingly strong feelings: that the
richer nations were not prepared to take seriously the developing
nations' plea for change; that their case was not being presented sympa-
thetically in the Western media, if indeed it was being presented at all;
and that the Western media were being used, that is, manipulated as

"instruments" for defending and promoting Western interests. Hence, the interconnection between the two seemingly separate issues of NIEO and the free flow of information.

The Western mass media without doubt has devoted comparatively little space either to reporting the NIEO debate or to discussing its importance; insofar as it was discussed (mainly in the small number of internationally minded American and European publications or in the minority interest radio and television programs), the treatment was largely devoted to explaining and justifying Western positions. As a result, the Third World felt that it had no platform in the Western world.

The blame for this increasingly was laid to the role of the major international news agencies, which were accused of exerting a monopolist stranglehold over the flow of news; of distorting news, or serving the economic and political interests of Western powers; and of blocking the development of rival news services operated by non-Western agencies.

The Role of the Western News Agencies

The operation of the four big Western agencies is largely based on the economy of scale and on the notion that the clients' interests come first—a consideration that naturally puts the most rewarding market sectors in the forefront of agency editors' minds. Few individual newspapers in the West, not to mention the Third World, can now afford to support their correspondents abroad (a foreign post is estimated to cost between $100,000 and $150,000 a year). And those newspapers that do continue to maintain foreign bureaus, such as the *New York Times* and the *Washington Post,* have established minor transnational agencies in order to offset their costs by reselling foreign news as supplementary services to the big agencies: even so, they are obliged to rent the wire facilities of the major agencies in order to "hook into" the most profitable sectors of the market.

In recent years, the transformation of print technology in the West has been inextricably linked with, and in fact preceded by, the new technologies in news servicing. Hundreds of newspapers have abandoned hard copy, along with compositors, for high-speed wire systems, computer retrieval banks, and VDT editing. Once the investment has been made, the new hardware must be used.

In most cases, the cost of the hardware has squeezed out alternative modes of servicing. The "bottom line" consideration is unassailable for most newspapers struggling with inflation and with the traditionally recalcitrant economics of the industry: it is cheaper to subscribe to one agency representing eight foreign bureaus than to subsidize a single reporter abroad. This also is the case in picture servicing. And what is true of the relatively wealthy newspapers in the West is even truer of most Third World newspapers.

Associated Press (AP), founded in 1848 as a cooperative of 6 publishers in New York, today includes 1,300 newspaper member publishers with some 10,000 subscribing organizations, transmits approximately 17 million words a day to 10,000 member agencies, and employs journalists in 110 countries. AP executives insist that their news values reflect the needs of subscribing managing editors rather than the monopolistic dictates of a clique of decisionmakers; these editors, needless to say, are American.

A consistent Third World criticism of the agencies, and of AP in particular, is that before being distributed, copy from the Third World goes to New York for processing (or "twisting"). Rosemary Righter reports a typical comment at a UNESCO conference in Florence in April 1977: "The control of news flow into the Latin American region is dominated by the United States wire services that systematically distort through selection and manipulation the image of the world outside presented to the Latin Americans through their papers."[2]

Yet AP and United Press International (UPI), both strong in Latin America, maintain that most of their bureaus in the area are run by nationals and that their transmission technology is hooked into the U.S. system in such a way that processing at the center is precluded.

AP is by tradition a nonprofitmaking organization: what small profit it does make derives from providing services to radio networks and overseas newspapers. AP claims to make no more than 1 percent of its total income from the Third World, while spending five times as much covering news events there.

UPI, which has been in operation for seventy years, transmits approximately 14 million words a day and maintains an exclusive picture service. Although it does not claim to be a nonprofitmaking organization, its executives are quick to point out that the news service, as opposed to the company's spin-offs, makes little, if any, money. It currently services about 7,000 subscribers in more than 90 countries and, like AP, provides extensive regional services run by nationals.

Reuters, which transmits more than 1.5 million words a day in 6 languages to 154 countries, has been in continuous operation for over 125 years, since it serviced clients by means of carrier pigeon. Basically a British and Commonwealth limited company registered in the United Kingdom and owned by four associations representing the national newspapers of the United Kingdom, the regional newspapers of the United Kingdom, and the newspapers of the Republic of Ireland, Australia, and New Zealand, it has 501 full-time journalists and 800 stringers around the world. The most profitable side of its business involves the sale of economic and financial information. AP—like UPI—executives deny that they make money out of selling news abroad. Reuters has strong regional services—particularly in Africa, where the relations forged in colonial times have survived—and cooperated with one of the first intergovernmental regional services in helping to establish CANA in the Caribbean.

Agence France Press (AFP) transmits more than 3 million words a day to 12,000 newspapers in 80 countries. It is a curious organization in that, although about 70 percent of its budget derives from a government subsidy, it enjoys editorial autonomy. AFP employs 171 journalists and more than 1,000 stringers in 100 bureaus around the world. Its executives claim that Third World coverage is a drain on the company's profits.

While the major services are clearly striving to be international in outlook and coverage, the market dictates that they serve the interests of the richest sectors, which in turn entails following the news values that reflect commonly agreed-on criteria of what is important. As one major magazine editor giving evidence at our Blenheim conference remarked: "People do not expect Pomona, Illinois, to be given the same treatment as Chicago."

Agency executives maintain that, commercial considerations aside, they try to do justice to Third World reporting. Many of them claim that they could pull out of the Third World tomorrow and not feel any financial pinch. UPI has in fact closed bureaus in several African countries.

All the same, from the point of view of the Third World, the major agencies represent alien, if not necessarily hostile, interests. The imbalance of coverage between the West and the Third World was recently cited by Sean MacBride, chairman of UNESCO's International Communications Commission: of the five largest news agency correspondents throughout the world, 34 percent are in the United States, 28 percent in Europe, 17 percent in Asia and Australia, 11 percent in Latin America, 6 percent in the Middle East, and 4 percent in Africa.

II/Four Areas of Confrontation

The View from the Third World

Many countries in the Third World complain that they are bombarded twenty-four hours a day, seven days a week by foreign news and information. Two-thirds of the world's information originates directly or indirectly in the United States; the rest comes, in roughly the following order of importance, from England, France, the Soviet Union, and China. The ubiquitous transistor radios (when not tuned in to local stations) carry information from the BBC, Voice of America, RFA (Paris), Deutschwelle (West Germany), Radio Free Europe, Radio Liberty, Radio Moscow, and Radio Peking. The great bulk of all television programs and films comes from the United States and England. American television exports amount to between 100,000 and 200,000 hours of programming annually. With very little international coverage in their local papers, most of it originating from foreign sources, Third World audiences depend for most of their information on imported magazines, especially *Time* and *Newsweek,* which together sell 830,000 copies a week in the Third World markets, and the *Reader's Digest;* the *Economist* is found on the desks of a high proportion of Third World decisionmakers. In the French-speaking areas of the Third World, the elite rely almost exclusively on *Le Monde* for their knowledge of the outside world. Against this massive input of Western information, Soviet and Chinese publications hardly rate as major sources of news and opinion. Although this state of affairs can be seen only to reflect the long historical connections between most of the new nations and the major Western powers, it is hardly surprising that a strong reaction should have set in among the younger developing nations against the virtual monopoly of the powerful Western mass media.

The Third World is perhaps even more pluralistic than the Western community. Its members include countries as wedded to Marxism, such as Cuba, Vietnam, Angola, and Mozambique, as to capitalism, such as South Korea, Ivory Coast, Brazil, and Singapore. They include countries striving to maintain systems of parliamentary democracy, such as India, Malaysia, Jamaica, Mexico, and Mauritius, and some that are little more than tyrannies, such as Uganda, Equatorial Guinea, and Haiti. Their levels of economic development are strikingly different—ranging from oil-rich states, such as Iran, Libya, Saudi Arabia, Nigeria, Kuwait, and Venezuela, to the world's poorest nations, such as Upper Volta, Rwanda, and Mali. Some already are well on their way to becoming industrialized, such as India, Mexico, and Singapore; the others have hardly reached the first level of industrial modernization, such as Botswana, Rwanda, and Oman. Moreover, many Third World countries are actively hostile to each other, such as Somalia vs. Ethiopia; Algeria vs. Morocco; Libya vs. Egypt; Egypt vs. Syria; Uganda vs. Tanzania; India vs. Pakistan.

While we must not lose sight of the multifaceted nature of the Third World when we evaluate its degree of collective interest in pursuing such issues as the free flow of information, there is nevertheless considerable validity in portraying this diversity of states as having essentially different interests from those of either the West or the Soviet bloc and of having a distinctive attitude deriving from recent colonial experience, mainly as Western (that is, white) dependencies. In casting off their former political and economic dependency—and inferior status—they share certain interests vis-à-vis the industrialized nations and hold similar views. Until only a few decades ago, all were completely tied into the Western economic, political, and social system: all lines led to the West. Now, it is felt, all lines still lead *from* the West—not only is the flow of information one-way, it also is one-sided: the Western side.

Third World criticisms of the Western media have been stated in various ways over the past seven years, but perhaps the most succinct ''definition'' was formulated at the New Delhi nonaligned meeting in July 1976:

Global information flows are marked by serious inadequacy and imbalance, that the means of communicating information are concentrated in a few countries, and that the great majority of countries are reduced to being passive recipients of information which is disseminated from a few centres.

This situation perpetuates the colonial era of dependence and domination. It confines judgments and decisions on what should be known and how it should be made known, *into the hands of the few*. In a situation where the means of information are dominated and monopolised by a few, freedom of these few to propagate information in the manner of their choosing and the virtual denial to the rest of the right to inform and be informed objectively and accurately.[1]

The four major international news agencies—AP, UPI, Reuters, and AFP—are virtually the only sources of international news in the Third World.

It is commonly held that the end of colonialism has not changed the hierarchical nature of the transnational power structure, which still ensures the dominance of the West and the subjugation, even exploitation, of the former colonies.

There is a tremendous inequality between the resources of most developing countries and those of major transnational news agencies—perceived in the Third World as representing powerful alien interests. It has been estimated that a single day's resources of one of the four major Western news agencies exceed the total annual expenditures of many of the smaller Asian and African countries.[2]

Competition is virtually inconceivable. Where they have attempted to compete, Third World news services claim that the transnationals have utilized the built-in advantages of West-centered communications links to transmit their messages cheaply and more quickly. Moreover, because the smaller agencies have fewer subscribers, their services are more expensive. In India, for example, they are available for only two to four hours at night, while the Western agencies operate around the clock.

It is not only their size and dominance that are held against the American, British, and French news services; it is also the kind of information they transmit. Even a moderate critic, like Narinder K. Aggarwala, an Indian journalist employed by the UN Development Program, complains that "the style, the content, and the treatment of practically all the news flowing in and out of the Third World reflect the personality, preference, and the needs of the Western media."[3]

In the context of the north-south confrontation over the NIEO, the Western news agencies are felt to project almost exclusively the northern perspective of world news. This suspicion about Western news agencies serving particular vested interests finds expression in such statements as those made by Louis Penalaver, Venezuela's minister of information: "Why," he asked, "should we rely exclusively on foreign news services, which represent powerful economic interests, to hear about our own neighbors?"

The criticisms of the major Western news agencies also are frequently expressed in ideological terms by an influential group of media men (not all of them necessarily Marxists) who are frequently quoted in UNESCO reports and who also serve as special personnel at regional conferences sponsored by UNESCO.

To Juan Somavia, who is associated with Mexico's Latin American Institute for Transnational Studies, the present communications system is "a vehicle for transmitting values and life-styles to Third World countries which stimulate the type of consumption and the type of society necessary to the transnational system as a whole. Politically, it defends the status quo, where this is its own interest; economically, it creates the conditions for the transnational expansion of capital."[4]

Critics such as Somavia regard the Western-dominated communications system as being operated as part of a "conspiracy" against the developing nations. Moreover, because the Western-controlled news agencies see news in commercial terms, they are held to have a built-in discrimination against news events that cannot be "sold," and at the same time, they tend to distort the presentation of events "to make them more marketable."

Even those critics who do not share Somavia's views agree with him that, on the whole, Western newspapermen see "aberrations" as "news," which in turn "obliges" them to "sensationalize."[5] This Western attitude toward what is considered "news" is responsible, so the argument goes, for the disproportionate amount of coverage of wars, disease, crime, corruption, and other sensational subjects. As a result, there is a steady underreporting—not to say, undermining—of the cultural, economic, and political progress being made by the developing world.[6]

Thus, the Western media are felt to be contributing toward building up a one-sided and distorted view of actual conditions in the Third World. This harmful view is seen to be imposed not only on Western audiences but also on the Third World since so many of its own papers publish only what is transmitted by the Western news agencies. The cumulative effect of this view is held to be psychologically harmful to development.

Dr. Richard Hoggart, assistant director-general of UNESCO from 1970 to 1975, is among those who have urged that the West needs "to appreciate better the force of the resentment in the developing world at the developed world's predominance in mass media production." He goes on to say:

It is claimed that this mass of material coming in from outside is both erasing traditional cultures and inhibiting the emergence of authentic cultural changes[for instance, in newly created states]. There is no clear proof that this is in fact happening, nor indeed any proof that it is not; so the new nations are right to show concern. They go further and argue that the more powerful nations provide total "ways of seeing the world," present through their news-gathering machines and with the claim that that news is objective and ideology-free, a view of the nature, order and significance of events which is in reality determined by Western assumptions as to what constitutes news, and what doesn't. This recalls the debate now in progress within Great Britain about the "structuring of reality" by our own internal news processes. The two arguments are indeed closely related, but that by the developing world is more comprehensive.[7]

The Third World's primary concern with economic and social development has produced attitudes toward the role of the mass media that are strongly at variance with the traditional Western ideas about the role of the press, radio, and television. It is this basic conflict of attitude toward the mass media that lies at the center of the tension between the West and the Third World.

The idea of harnessing the mass media to national purposes is, predictably, repugnant to Western journalists and consonant with the approach of the Communist nations; thus, it sometimes seems that the Third World's stand in the free-flow-of-information controversy is "Communist-inspired." This view is strongly resented by spokesmen of the Third World, who argue that a new style of journalism, one that asserts that good news is just as newsworthy as bad news, is essential to promoting national development policies. Indian journalist Dilip Mukerjee has gone so far as to demand a complete break with the Western philosophy of journalism:

> Our need is urgent and acute: we belong to societies which are in the process of restructuring and reshaping themselves. In our environment there is, and there will be for a long time to come, much that is ugly and distasteful. If we follow the Western norm, we will be playing up *only those dark spots,* and thus helping unwittingly to erode the faith and confidence without which growth and development are impossible. . . .[8]

Those who follow Mukerjee's line insist that the logical consequence of the need to gear the media to the purposes of national development programs may (or should) involve controlling the flow of information from abroad. On this issue, however, there are sharply different opinions. If the "objective reporter" is to play the role of social analyst and educator, where, asks Shashi Tharoor, is the thin line to be drawn between education and propaganda?[9] Since the "correct" development policy is decided by governments, should journalists accept their governments as the sole arbiters of what is to be communicated?

Hilary Ng'weno, a Kenyan editor, insists that a sharp distinction be drawn between the flow of information across national boundaries and the "more important" question of the flow of information within national boundaries.[10] He describes as "dangerous" the views of those who prescribe government control of the press as "the cure for the ills which afflict the press in Third World countries."

To sum up: the Third World nations generally believe that there is no free flow of information through the international communications system, that in fact the flow is almost entirely one-way; that the domination of the communications system by the West results in the projection of an inadequate and distorted image of Third World development not only to the international community but also to, and among, themselves; that they are subject to a transnational system of cultural imperialism; that their own development process is harmed by this unbalanced information about their affairs; and that all of the above amount almost to a physical barrier to their development programs. For all these reasons, then, the Third World is seeking to restructure the existing system of international communications.

There is a fairly broad measure of agreement on these fundamental criticisms and aspirations, but there is far less agreement as to which measures to take in order to change this state of affairs.

Meanwhile, Third World countries have taken a number of steps to establish a network of national news agencies, regional news agencies, and a news agency "pool" of nonaligned countries. They have developed their own system of satellites and have taken other measures to remedy weaknesses in the infrastructure of their communications system, such as initiating training programs for media professionals and technicians.

Summary of Moves to Establish Regional News Agencies

After a meeting of nonaligned countries in Algeria in September 1973, it was recommended that a Third World news agency be created to counteract the imbalance in the flow of international news put out by the Western news agencies. The recommendation was further elaborated at UNESCO-sponsored meetings in Lima (August 1975), Tunis (March 1976), and Mexico City (May 1976). Yugoslavia offered the facilities of Tanjug, its government-owned news agency, to provide a news "pool" for Third World countries. Some fifty countries now participate in feeding selected news items into the pool.

The idea of a Third World pool was carried forward at the nonaligned conference in New Delhi (July 1976), where a constitution was drawn up providing for suitable bodies to implement and supervise the pool. There was considerable pressure against proposed government control and financing of such a news pool, and the constitution provides for the pool to be a "self-financing activity" in which "none of the pool-participating agencies has a dominant role."

India merged its four national news agencies in 1976 into a single agency called Samachar, with a view to playing a role in the nonaligned pool comparable to Tanjug's. Mrs. Gandhi's "emergency" overtook events, but the repressive measures she instituted against the press were rescinded after she lost the general election in March 1977. The future of Samachar is yet to be decided.

In April 1977, representatives from sixteen Arab and thirty African countries voted to study proposals for a joint Arab-African news agency.

In November 1977, the information ministers of the Organization of African Unity decided in Kampala to establish a Pan-African News Agency. As a preliminary step, they formed an Inter-Governmental Council for Information in Africa. This decision marked the culmination of fourteen years of discussions on the need to establish such an agency.

In April 1978, the Inter-Governmental Council for the Coordination of Information from Nonaligned Countries met in Havana and approved recommendations for upgrading their common news pool and for solving their communications problems. This move represents a further attempt to follow up the decision taken at the 1976 meeting of the nonaligned countries to "decolonize" information about developing countries. The proposals put forward included establishing additional national news agencies, establishing training courses for journalists, increasing exchanges between radio and television networks, lowering communication tariffs for news transmissions, and improving communications facilities.

In March 1978, the Cooperation Committee of the broadcasting organizations of the nonaligned countries decided in Baghdad to develop exchange programs to train personnel and to form "program banks," that is, regional centers for the exchange of radio and television programs. They also discussed possibilities for using satellites for broadcasting. And in 1977 in Sarajevo, the Committee for Cooperation was formed by the radio and television bodies of nineteen nonaligned countries.

The View from the West

Mention has already been made of the pluralist nature of interests and attitudes in the Third World, but it must be pointed out that the West also is pluralistic. On both sides of this debate, there is a serious danger of oversimplification in writing about "the Western view," the "Western press," and so forth. The fact is that Western attitudes toward the issues raised in the discussion over the free flow of information are fairly sharply divided between those who see the Third World (Soviet bloc–UNESCO) campaign as a threat to press freedom everywhere and those who admit that there are serious flaws in the present situation that should be remedied. Even between these two broad viewpoints, there are striking differences of approach.

The outstanding exposition of the first of these viewpoints, that the Third World's demands are a threat to free information, was stated in 1976 by Leonard R. Sussman. He saw the transnational news services based in Western countries—"long the acknowledged reporters of worldwide events and movements"—as being challenged by "diversely-motivated" nations in the Third World that, nevertheless, maintain "an underlying unity to the attacks"; these are "readily exploited by the Marxist apparatus of the Soviet Union . . . in order to advance Marxism's political and economic goal: the ultimate defeat everywhere of free market economies, non-Marxist political systems, and their matching 'bourgeois' cultures."[11]

The Zurich-based International Press Institute also sees serious reasons for Western concern that Third World news agencies could constitute "a very real threat to the freedom of the press and the free flow of news" because the majority of Third World governments have full control of the mass media in their countries and restrict the freedom of expression in various ways. "Hence, a news agency pool or regional news agencies could become merely exchanges of official government statements. Secondly, Western news agencies and reporters may be excluded. . . . Such a development constitutes an interference with the free flow of information."[12]

By and large, though, the controversy has succeeded in making the West aware that there may be some serious problems in the international communications system, with the result that the internationally minded Western media have begun to consider positive ways of meeting some of the Third World's criticisms. Fears that news agencies to rival the West's "big four" might be developed, restricting the freedom of international reporters, have to some extent been allayed by studies made of the first such potential rival organized by the Yugoslav news agency, Tanjug. The best study is that made by Edward T. Pinch of the U.S. State Department, in which he concludes that common ground exists between the two sides:

> Western journalists do not have to accept all Third World criticism of their coverage of events in order to recognize legitimate complaints regarding the superficiality or irrelevance of some of it. Third World officials, in turn, should be able to aspire to reducing the imbalance in their own media

capabilities without seeking to inhibit the communications capacities of others.[13]

Pinch's conclusion regarding the Tanjug operation of a pool of nonaligned nations is that it can become a "threat" (that is, a serious competitor) to the major Western news agencies only if it adopts the same "philosophy as well as hardware." Such a threat, he maintains, is one that would be "indeed welcome."

Most Western journalists with international experience are concerned that Third World countries will make it more difficult for foreign correspondents to carry out their assignments. As an example, they cite the growing tendency of countries in the developing world to emulate the well-established practices of the Soviet bloc countries in carefully monitoring resident and visiting correspondents, refusing them visas, restricting their freedom of movement or their opportunities for independent access to information sources, and even expelling them if they write anything deemed unfavorable by the regime in power.

These are well-grounded fears, but they do not apply to Western journalists alone. Many Third World journalists experience similar difficulties in working in a number of non-Western countries—and even more find it difficult, and sometimes impossible, to work as independent journalists in their own countries. There are scores of Africans, Arabs, Asians, and Latin Americans living and working abroad because they are not allowed to function freely at home.

The problem of the free flow of information is not only lateral, as between countries; it also is internal, and this element has largely been overlooked in previous arguments about the flow of information. It is therefore encouraging that special attention was focused on this problem by Sean MacBride, president of UNESCO's International Commission for the Study of Communication Problems. In his inaugural address to the commission in Paris on December 14, 1977, he stressed that:

> There is an obvious link between communications on the national and international levels. To isolate one from the other, to treat them separately, as often happens, would not only be a mistake, but is really impossible. So many complaints and criticisms on the international sphere, justified or exaggerated, about monopolies and imbalances in communication, or about the role of transnational companies or the neglect of cultural identity and heredity, are certainly connected with what is often taking place inside various countries.

Most working journalists in Western and Third World countries welcome MacBride's proposal to study the "internal flow" of information, but it is unlikely to be favored by regimes operating within "closed

societies." As Mort Rosenblum correctly states: "No government any-
where enjoys energetic probing by the Press."[14] The point is developed
by Hilary Ng'weno:

> Many young countries have fragile political structures that cannot with-
> stand endless scrutiny by the news media of the shortcomings of those in
> power or the failures of economic and social development programs. Unfor-
> tunately for the cause of free communication of ideas, it is precisely the
> negative and unseemly side of life which many Western reporters and news
> media tend to harp upon when dealing with developments in young coun-
> tries. Coups, corruption, poverty and calamities are the staple diet dished out
> by many news agencies in their coverage of Third World countries.[15]

Yet it is precisely because local journalists often are prevented from
probing conditions at home that the role of the foreign journalist is such
an indispensable feature in the process of ensuring a flow of information
based on nongovernmental sources. This is a subject to which very little
attention has been paid in UNESCO studies.

It is surely not enough to complain about foreign journalists' reports
without at the same time stressing the importance of their being allowed
greater freedom to do their job properly. While it is too much to suppose
that the freedom allowed foreign journalists in Western countries can be
achieved at this stage in the Third World or Soviet bloc countries, this
aim should nevertheless be pursued. And this, it can be argued, also is
an interest of Third World countries because opposition elements in
"closed societies" generally find that their views and criticisms, and the
actual state of affairs in their countries, can only, or mainly, be con-
veyed to the outside world (and often inside their own countries) through
the work of foreign reporters. For example, reports appearing in Western or African newspapers about events in Uganda are widely disseminated inside that country through xeroxed leaflets.

To sum up: While Western attitudes toward the Third World's challenge are polarized between those who tend to see the issues largely in
ideological terms and those who accept that, although much of the
criticism may be extravagantly stated, there is nevertheless a real problem worthy of detailed examination; that Western and non-Western
ideas about the role of the mass media diverge, often quite sharply; that
the development of Third World news agencies is inevitable and could
make an important contribution to promoting a two-way flow of information, provided they are not simply controlled by governments or
accompanied by unfair restrictions on other news agencies or foreign
journalists; and that there is a need to examine the internal flow of
information as an essential element in ensuring an adequate international flow of information.

The Role of the Soviet Union

In 1972, the Soviet Union sponsored a resolution in UNESCO calling for the drafting of "Fundamental Principles Governing the Use of News Media." Although UNESCO had been engaged since the early 1950s in studying problems of international communications (see below), after the Soviet resolution was adopted the debate on these issues became increasingly entangled with ideological questions about the role of the mass media in society.

The Soviet model of the proper use of the mass media has an obvious pragmatic, although not necessarily ideological, appeal for many Third World countries, including those that are not themselves Marxist and that may in fact be strongly anti-Communist. Their policies, like those of the Soviets, are primarily development-oriented; the majority are in many respects "closed societies" in that they reject the idea of political pluralism and still are engaged in the difficult transitional stages of independence, with the problem of having both to establish viable institutions and to achieve internal stability.

It is axiomatic that a truly free press can exist only in an "open society" with legally recognized pluralist political institutions. In societies where all the levers of power, control, and influence are in the hands of a single party or a dominant political center, it is idle to suppose that a weapon as potent as a critical press or radio can be tolerated; at best, it will be subjected to strict government surveillance and control.

Thus, in the present stage of their transformation, many, if not most, Third World countries share the Communists' basic premise that "the government and the people are one, that the state represents the true interests of the masses, and that all the media should be centrally controlled and directed, informing and educating the people about the policies of the government." Education, information, and propaganda are all held to be equally the function of the mass media, and there can be no countercenter of information or propaganda. This applies not only to the internal flow of information but also to the external flow.

But while the Soviet model makes some obvious appeal to the newer nations, very few are as centrally controlled as the Communist states are, and many happen to share a democratic aspiration, however short of precept their practices may fall.

The differences between Soviet ideas and those of a substantial part of the Third World clearly emerged at the UNESCO general conference held in Nairobi in 1976. The central issue was over a Soviet-sponsored article in the draft "Declaration on Fundamental Principles Governing the Use of the Mass Media in Strengthening Peace and International

Understanding and in Combatting War Propaganda, Racism and Apartheid.'' The debate turned largely on Article XII, which declared that "states are responsible for the activities in the international sphere of all mass media under their jurisdiction.''

All the Western delegates took the view that for governments to supervise and control the activities of their subjects constituted a direct infringement of freedom of speech and information. The proposal, in fact, amounted to applying at the international level what the centrally organized states practiced in their own countries. Such an idea is obviously incompatible with Western concepts of press freedom.

After a lengthy debate, which pointed up the differences not only between the Western and Communist nations but also within the Third World, consideration of the draft was postponed for two years.

It is this drift toward accepting the need for governmental control over the mass media, occurring within the framework of UNESCO, that has brought the international conflict over the flow of information to its present pitch.

Although the issues were somewhat defused as a result of the decision at Nairobi not to endorse the draft, the central problem remains: a sharp dichotomy between those who believe that government control over the mass media is both desirable and necessary and those who see the proposal as being in conflict with the Universal Declaration of Human Rights, which, inter alia, guarantees freedom of thought and the free flow of information.

Thus, the international community remains undecided between two fundamentally irreconcilable views about the nature of the freedom of communication.

The issues at stake in the Nairobi conference were summed up at the time by Hilary Ng'weno:

> If most Third World delegates at the UNESCO general assembly should end up endorsing the UNESCO media proposals and thus side with the Soviet Union and Eastern bloc countries on the issue of Press freedom, it will be understandable. Most of the delegates at the conference are government functionaries with little or no first-hand working knowledge of the media. Like most government functionaries all over the world, their concern is not with imparting information but with influencing people. For them, information is not information until its probable impact on select audiences has been ascertained. There is good information or information fit for human consumption, and there is bad information—that which must not be fed to the public. The truth or untruth of the information is of secondary importance to government officials. Indeed, sometimes, the greater the truth the greater the desire on the part of the government functionary to delay its dissemination, especially if the truth happens to be unpalatable. And it matters not whether the functionary is a Haldeman or Erlichman serving a Nixon beleaguered by

Watergate scandals, or a party hack in Moscow trying to conceal the fact that dozens of Soviet citizens may have lost their lives in an Aeroflot air crash somewhere in Siberia. It will be understandable that such officials will lean towards supporting measures for the greater government control of the Press. Such control makes their job easier, but only temporarily.

In the final analysis, government control of the Press leads to the kinds of distortions which Third World nations are complaining of with regard to the influence and practice of Western news agencies. These distortions cloud the vision of leaders and make them prone to ill-considered decisions, with sometimes fatal consequences for a country. A government-controlled Press is by its very nature a mouth-piece of those in power. Like the piper it learns to sing those tunes dearest to whoever is paying, and the numerous upheavals in Third World nations over the past ten years prove beyond any shadow of a doubt that what is politically fashionable today need have no appeal whatsoever to incoming regimes bent on establishing fresh legitimacy for their illegal seizure of political power.

Ng'weno was not the only Third World journalist to speak up for press freedom; his views were echoed in many parts of the developing world. A Nigerian commentator reported on Radio Lagos on November 30, 1976:

Members of the UNESCO conference argued that government control of the Press was certainly not a cure for the ills of the mass media in the Third World countries, nor would it help the free flow of information. It was obvious that, if adopted, the draft declaration would have the effect of fettering the freedom of foreign newsmen operating across national boundaries.

Besides, the imposition of regulations as implied in the draft declaration, restricting the dissemination of domestic news abroad or to state-controlled news services, would amount to placing curbs on the free flow of information. The Soviet-inspired draft declaration was ultimately shelved because of the view of the majority of the UNESCO conference that the correct solution to the problem of the developing countries lies in measures which will give people the greatest possible diversity of opinions and to allow them to communicate easily with one another.

The Role of UNESCO

The United Nations Educational, Scientific, and Cultural Organization has played a central—and controversial—role in promoting discussions and ideas about how best to promote freedom of information and in focusing attention on the present imbalance in the flow of news. Like other UN specialized agencies, UNESCO has in recent years increasingly become a platform for Third World voices in international affairs. Not surprisingly in view of its functions, it also has become an arena for Western-Eastern ideological conflict.

On certain sensitive issues, for example, the Arab stand against Israel and in favor of recognition of the Palestinian Liberation Organization, the Third World and the Soviet countries have successfully combined to outvote the Western nations. This alliance has produced strains within the organization, which have become focused on the flow of information studies by UNESCO. These studies, as Shashi Tharoor has perceptively described them, "provide an intellectual rationale" for many of the Third World's nascent feelings about the Western press and transnational news agencies.

UNESCO's interest in the communications field dates back to the early 1950s and derives from the principle in its 1945 charter that deals with the free flow of information and the pursuit of objective truth. It produced its first study in 1953—an analysis of the flow of one week's news, a comparative study of seven major dailies in the world, and a survey of the structure and operations of news agencies. A second study, in 1956, dealt with the problems of transmitting press messages. By 1961, UNESCO had come to identify the major Western news agencies as "one of the vital factors in the flow of information."

Until the end of the 1960s, UNESCO's work had been mainly of two kinds: investigative and practical. It was a UNESCO-sponsored conference in Bangkok in 1961 that led to the creation of the Organization of Asian News Agencies; a similar conference in Santiago in 1962 produced a recommendation to establish a regional news agency for Latin America; and a conference in Tunis in 1963 proposed the creation of a Union of African News Agencies. Thus, the main practical result of UNESCO's activities has been in promoting ideas about the importance of creating regional news agencies in the Third World.

UNESCO activities attracted little controversy until two resolutions were adopted, one in 1970 and the other in 1972. The first was a directive from UNESCO's general conference to "examine communications policies"; the second was the Soviet-sponsored resolution calling for the drafting of a declaration on fundamental principles governing the use of the mass media.

The essentially Third World focus of UNESCO's approach to the free flow of information is exemplified by a summary of the main results of its work published in the UNESCO *Chronicler* early in 1970. It stressed three major elements:

- That the developing countries and the rest of the international community "have become conscious of the one-sidedness of the flow of information."

- That the developing countries have begun to articulate their own demands "for a more equal access and participation in the world flow of news and media programs as part of the search for a New International Economic Order based upon a better distribution of resources and justice."

• That the least developed countries have become "alarmed" at the growing information gap between north and south and that "their image in the world at large is formed by media originating from, and influenced by, other cultural values and, sometimes, ideologies."

This presentation of the problems of the flow of information established the boundaries within which the international debate has been conducted ever since. It helped to set the scene for a confrontation between the Third World and the West, and it made the main target for its criticisms the Western-based transnational news agencies.

With the adoption of the Soviet-sponsored resolutions of 1972, this debate acquired a new ideological dimension—West vs. East. The nature of the debate has been admirably summed up by Richard Hoggart, who witnessed the sharpening of the controversy:

Year after year in this decade, the Soviet Union has put down resolutions at all the relevant UN conferences about the dangers of "uncontrolled" growth in mass media activity. The formulation is usually that, in view of the great power of these media, it is the duty of sovereign States to ensure that they are not used for "corrupting" ends; and, in particular, that States should agree not to transmit "undesirable material" across each other's frontiers. It is of no use to point out that in open societies governments do not usually exercise this type of control of the mass media; the resolutions continue, with the phrasing only marginally altered.

Self-evidently, this is an aspect of the general Soviet fear of the free expression and circulation of opinion. In this instance, it takes on a special edge precisely because Soviet officials are shrewd enough to recognize that the Western powers are exceptionally effective in using mass media in attractive, ingratiating, attention-catching ways.

This fear has been sharpened by the arrival of satellites. Mr. Gromyko has spoken strongly on the theme at the UN General Assembly in New York; and since 1972 the Soviets have been even more than usually active in the drafting of an international instrument on satellite use, in particular seeking provisions to ensure that they are not used to carry "degrading" commercial material, and that no State should direct satellite broadcast into another State's territory except with its agreement. The resultant *Declaration of Guiding Principles for the Use of Satellite Broadcasting for the Free Flow of Information, the Extension of Education and the Development of Cultural Exchanges* (1972) asserts:

"Satellite broadcasting shall respect the sovereignty and equality of all States. . . . The objective of satellite broadcasting for the free flow of information is to ensure the widest possible dissemination, among the peoples of the world, of news of all countries, developed and developing alike. . . . Cultural programmes, while promoting the enrichment of all cultures, should respect the distinctive character, the value and dignity of each, and the right of all countries and peoples to preserve their cultures as part of the common heritage of mankind.''

That deeply self-contradictory formulation (it speaks for free-but-controlled communication) is, it will be seen at once, likely to sound recognisable chords of disquiet—and will seem also to seek to allay them— in the breasts of those who govern developing countries. Thus, the Soviet Union once again allies herself with anti-imperialism, against the former colonial powers, on behalf of the integrity of individual cultures. Which seems even more than usually odd when one sets it against the controls on national political self-consciousness within the satellite and absorbed countries, or, indeed, against the restrictions on comment under which Finland labours as a condition of her independence. On the other hand, the developed countries should recognise more that satellite development has been and is being far too much defined by profit-making rather than by public considerations and needs.[16]

However, the disputes were not only north vs. south or west vs. east; the differences they produced within the Third World itself reflected its pluralist character. These differences surfaced most clearly at UNESCO's 1976 Nairobi conference and at a UNESCO-sponsored conference held in San José, Costa Rica, in July 1976. (The San José conference was scheduled to have been held in Ecuador, but its government refused to act as host after the Inter-American Press Association and the Inter-American Association of Broadcasters had publicly criticized the tone of some of the recommendations in UNESCO reports proposing strong government controls over the flow of news.)

The tone of the San José conference was set in the keynote address by UNESCO's director-general, Ahmadou-Mahtar M'Bow. He declared that the establishment of an NIEO ''requires new concepts in the flow of information,'' and he went on to say that UNESCO was ''absolutely in favor of freedom of information.'' But, he added, ''when mass communication media instill standards of values alien to any given region they threaten to eradicate or nullify that region's own values.'' He described freedom of expression as ''meaningless'' when newspapers are controlled by small groups or by families who deny ''access and participation'' to the people in general and when ''the international flow of news is controlled by a few industrialised countries.''

The final recommendations of the San José conference considerably modified the language, and rejected some of the key ideas, of the UNESCO experts; a proposed code of ethics for reporters was scrapped, and a clause was inserted for setting up national and regional news agencies ''to ensure that its establishment will in no way impair the free operation of existing agencies or their future development.'' But several clauses were adopted that implied government control of the media through the development of national communication policies. Although it was recommended that governments include ''all sectors concerned'' in formulating their national communications and information policies, they were nevertheless left with the power to determine the ''rights and responsibilities'' of the communicators.

After the Nairobi conference, UNESCO established a new International Commission for the Study of Communication Problems under the chairmanship of Irish lawyer and statesman Sean MacBride, formerly secretary-general of the International Commission of Jurists, chairman of Amnesty International, and secretary-general of the UN Commission for Namibia.

III/The Arguments and Issues

Is the Western Press Beyond Criticism?

Summarizing a list of Western press virtues, Peter Galliner, director of the International Press Institute (IPI) in Zurich, wrote: "The attractions of the Western model are the self-evident high standards of reporting, the relative objectivity and accuracy of information as well as freedom from any particular government line."[1]

This is the attractive side of the Western press, and most of us practicing journalism in the West believe that it holds largely true much of the time. There is another, less flattering image, however, and it has been described not only by critics outside our economic and political system but also by some distinguished figures within it.

Thirty years ago, George Orwell complained: "Any writer or journalist who wants to retain his integrity finds himself thwarted by the general drift of society rather than by active persecution. The sort of things that are working against him are the concentration of the Press in the hands of a few rich men, the grip of monopoly on radio and the films. . . ."[2]

Orwell was, of course, an idealistic writer with very high standards of journalistic integrity, and he was writing at a time when newspapers still were largely owned by "press barons"; but the darker view also has been depicted by some hardened media businessmen such as Cecil King, former chairman of IPC, Britain's biggest publisher, who wrote in a report to the British Council: "The British Press is, in fact, censored. Not directly; not openly by decree. But by the arbitrary operation of a series of loosely drawn laws which make it hazardous in the extreme for newspapers to comment or even report on a number of issues of vital public importance."

The point is that the Western model is open to criticism, even if—by Western standards—it is less flawed than models in closed societies.

49

The criticism has ranged from accusations of fundamental flaws in the system, such as those cited by Orwell, to the factual evidence that has recently been produced on worldwide manipulation of the press by the Central Intelligence Agency.

To quote one (by now familiar) item in the series of allegations: "According to the report of the Senate Committee, millions of dollars were spent by the CIA to produce a stream of anti-Allende stories, editorials and broadcasts throughout Latin America. A CIA propaganda assessment obtained by the committee, prepared shortly after Allende's election in September 1970, reported a 'continued replay of Chile theme materials' in a number of Latin American capitals with pickups by U.S. newspapers."[3]

The Western press also comes under fire from Marxist theorists, inside the West as well as outside, who see our media "model" as an important weapon in the West's master plan to subjugate the world. The Marxist analyses have been extensively set down in such books as Herbert Schiller's *Mass Communications and American Empire* (1969), Allan Well's *Picture Tube Imperialism* (1972), and Jeremy Tunstall's *The Media Are American* (1977).

The Marxist critics tend to regard news services, newspapers, radio, and television as a single conspiracy. But the argument now seems to be concentrated on television. Herbert Schiller, for example, accused the United States of pacifying the poor nations by its communications know-how and policies. His thesis is that the United States handed its telecommunications satellite system over to the big electronics companies (ATT, ITT, and RCA) and then negotiated with the Western nations an INTELSAT arrangement giving the United States dominance of world communications, the aim being to beam American network television, complete with commercials, straight into domestic television sets around the world; the homogenization of world culture would thereby be complete—false-consciousness would be plugged via satellite into every home.

Allan Wells elaborates on American media "imperialism," specifically in Latin American television; he maintains that technology, programming, and financing always have been dominated by U.S. companies, that U.S. direct ownership is very substantial, and that World Vision, an "ominously" titled subsidiary of the U.S. national ABC network, plays a dominant role in the region. American advertising agencies not only produce most of the numerous commercial breaks but also sponsor, shape, and indeed determine the whole pattern of programming and importing from the United States. "Approximately 80 percent of the hemisphere's current programs—including *The Flintstones, I Love Lucy, Bonanza,* and *Route 66*—were produced in the United States," he asserts.

The most recent figures on television exports to Latin America, compiled by media sociologist Tapio Varis in 1974 (see his *Global Television*), show that Wells' overall figure of 80 percent is greatly exaggerated. Varis found that the television channels in the larger Latin American countries (such as Argentina, Colombia, and Mexico) relied on imports from between 10 and 39 percent of their programming. Only one out of seven Latin American countries in the Varis study imported 80 percent of its programming—Guatemala.

Jeremy Tunstall focuses his criticism on America's "cultural imperialism." The American media system, he says, "has the effect of muting political protest in much of the world; local and authentic culture in many countries is driven on to the defensive by homogenised American culture."[4]

Marxist critics accuse the Western press not only of distortion by massive conspiracy but also of direct alignment with the giant capitalist monopolies. As Marxist sociologist Paul Hoch puts it: "The point is that, in ninety-nine cases out of a hundred the *New York Times* will insist on the policy most in the interest of the corporate business class, without having to be lobbied, threatened or controlled. It is not just a case of evil military industrialists or international bankers 'dominating' the newspaper corporations. All of the major corporations really do have common class interests."[5]

The points need not be labored that there is an enormous difference between practical criticism and ideological criticism and that any kind of criticism is weak unless it can be backed up with evidence.

Answering a Criticism with a Countercriticism

The debate over the free flow of information and the Third World is commonly depicted as one between two monolithic and opposed sets of interests—the big Western agencies (notably, AP, UPI, Reuters, and AFP) and those of the developing countries.

Some influential Western newspapers and media institutions have accused the Third World countries and UNESCO of attacking press freedom and of favoring a Soviet-style media. Typical of the extreme countercriticism is an editorial by Robert U. Brown that appeared in *Editor and Publisher* in March 1976: "UNESCO is inducing Latin American governments to establish official news agencies," he announced. "Dictatorships of the Left and the Right have long known that control of the news flow as well as control of news media have been essential for self-perpetuation. . . . The tentacles of the censorship octopus spread."

Brown clearly suggests that there is a conspiracy afoot, and he assumes that government sponsorship automatically means state control and the exclusion of pluralism. The complaints of the Third World and the optimistic planning of new press pools were represented simply as attempts to combat a free flow of information.

Commenting on the UNESCO Costa Rica meeting aimed at establishing a regional news agency, David Adamson reflected in the London *Daily Telegraph* in July 1976 that it was deplorable how "former colonies want a free flow of air—but not of information." He went on to report that "among the 'jollier ideas' thrown out at San José was legalising the arrest of foreign correspondents if their employers published anything not to the taste of the country concerned."[6] This "jollier" idea was reported nowhere else, but its source was not entirely a mystery.

In the same piece, Adamson cited Peter Galliner as having accused the senior staff of UNESCO of being "strongly leftist" and "in support of the idea of government-controlled news." He went on to hint that the initial "idea" behind the San José conference "came from a directive drawn up by Russia and Byelorussia in 1972."

In a letter of complaint to the *Daily Telegraph* editor, Gunnar R. Naesselund, deputy assistant director-general, Sector of Culture and Communication of UNESCO, pointed out that the communication policies program stemmed from ideas "initiated among primarily representatives of developing countries as far back as 1968 and was first presented in the form of a General Conference Resolution in 1970." Naesselund also suggested that both Adamson's attack on the Third World news pool plans and UNESCO's encouragement had been influenced by a press handout, issued June 30, 1976, from Freedom House director Leonard R. Sussman, warning that at the forthcoming UNESCO conference on Communications Policies one of the "alternatives" posed would be the "exclusion, intimidation or hampering of free Press correspondents." The handout also stated that the conference papers presented the following three alternatives (the points, including phrases in quotes, are interpretations of UNESCO documents):

(a) Government-run news agencies "exclusively empowered" to disseminate information from outside the country.

(b) "Legal measures" to "provide a defense against the competition of journalists from the major international Press services. A reporter abroad could face arrest if his home office publishes views regarded as 'anti-State' in the place where correspondents are stationed."

(c) Nationalization of independent print and broadcast news agencies.

Naesselund's letter to the *Daily Telegraph* dealt mainly with the points raised in Adamson's article, but in an *aide memoire* released on July 30, he criticized the Freedom House press handout in greater detail. He went so far as to claim that the "alternatives" were a complete distortion of the sense of a paragraph that appears under the heading *A News Agency for Latin America and the Caribbean:*

> (c) Emphasis should be laid on the need for those governments in the region which participate in the establishment of the agency to take legal measures designed to afford protection and effective support for the operation of the institution and, hence, to provide a defence against the competition of agencies outside the region. These measures should include the fixing of preferential rates and the fixing of minimum percentages for media dissemination which could secure a minimum basis of viability for the operation of the regional agency.[7]

According to Naesselund, the idea was to reasonably protect the newly established regional agency during the running-in periods through preferential treatments, which are well known in other sectors of the economy. He further pointed out the sly substitution of "journalists" for "international agencies," making it seem that the "legal measures" would be directed against any roving correspondent trying to compete with the new agency.

It is necessary to cite this "quarrel" at some length in order to illustrate the need for caution when reading interpretations of UNESCO's policy toward information flow over the past decade; the same caution should be extended to monolithic-style statements made by the nonaligned countries on this issue.

Despite constant appeals to read the documents themselves, the ideas prevail that UNESCO is advocating "thought control" and that all nonaligned nations speak with one voice for government and strangle-of the media.

It is interesting that on August 21, 1976, two weeks after the publication of the *Daily Telegraph* article, a piece appeared in the London *Evening Standard* datelined Paris and headlined "UNESCO Defends State News Agencies." Freedom House was cited as the source, even though the piece carried an interview with a UNESCO official explaining that the point of their program was simply to have a news agency, whether it is government or privately owned.

A second familiar response to Third World criticism is that, if developing countries made themselves more accessible to Western journalists, there would be no problem of information flow. As Peter Galliner has commented: "What appears to many people in the Third World to be over-simplification and hostile interpretation of intricate political developments is, in many cases, due to the problems of geographical distance and frequently caused by the difficulties placed in the way of Western journalists in the very countries who complain the most."[8]

Citing a number of incidents where its journalists had been harassed in Third World countries over the past year, the Associated Press recently concluded that "the major obstacles AP encounters in collecting a factual global news report are restricted access, explicit or implicit censorship and pressure against correspondents . . . direct action against foreign correspondents is the most extreme and dangerous obstacle to free news coverage."[9]

The annual lists of incidents recording attacks on journalists and press freedom make for very somber reading. However, it is clear from surveys published by the International Press Institute and *Index* that the Third World does not have a monopoly on restricting journalists. In any case, to reply to the Third World with counterallegations does not advance the dialogue.

The game can be played by both sides, as was demonstrated by Clayton Kirkpatrick, chairman of the American Society of Newspaper Editors International Communication Committee. Referring to the allegation of CIA abuse of the global media, he said that, during a recent visit, "All Indian stringers for American news agencies were not trusted, were not given background information because people believe these stringers were not only serving UPI and AP but also CIA."[10]

Before any productive dialogue can take place, there must be an acknowledgment that there is indeed a criticism to answer—the sort of acknowledgment, perhaps, that appeared in a *Washington Post* editorial during the Nairobi conference in 1976:

> One does not have to accept Third World charges that Western news agencies are cultural and political predators in order to understand a country's reluctance to have its picture of the world, and the world's picture of it, drawn entirely by foreigners who are sometimes sympathetic and knowledgeable, sometimes not, but who nevertheless are foreigners.[11]

Another major block to constructive debate is the widely held assumption that the nonaligned news pools will inevitably mean a government-dominated media in the Third World, with the specter of propaganda and censorship on an Orwellian scale.

Any media organization funded by governments runs the risks of domination and interference, and while that danger must be faced and discussed, it should be viewed in perspective. Gerald Long, managing director of Reuters, has described the problem that newly independent countries encounter:

A country in Africa that rid itself of colonial government—set up a government of its own—probably found, when it took over, that it had no media at all. There may have been a colonial newspaper in the capital. That went, because the regime went. And everything in the media there—the whole information system—had to be constructed from nothing, from zero.

Now, what point is there in saying to a country in that situation: you must have a fully-fledged Press freedom set-up, such as there exists in France, or in the United States? It's meaningless for that country to say that. It can't do that and it doesn't want to. Its priorities are different.

So if one looks, then, at how that country handles information, how it permits people to come in and report, how it permits information to be sent out of the country, information disseminated within the country, then, I think that a number of those countries that are of very recent foundation have an admirable record. I think they have faced up to great difficulties and the temptations to be very authoritarian very often in the information area extremely well and have shown great responsibility. And I refuse to say things that would condemn them in a blanket sort of way.[12]

Long went on to comment that any government bent on controlling its information was going to control it, and that the creation of a news pool would therefore be "an effect and not a cause." The decision to control information, he concluded, "exists quite independently of any desire to exchange the news—which they then control."

The extent to which government sponsorship constitutes a danger to the freedom, truth, and accuracy of the media clearly depends on the number of checks and balances in a given situation. Should one automatically dismiss Agence France Press and the BBC as suspect on the ground that they are both government sponsored?

Fears that a giant state-sponsored agency is about to challenge the flows and patterns of international news material are certainly not shared by the Western agencies themselves. An AP statement announced: "[We] believe that the more journalistic voices the world hears, the better informed it will be. For that reason, AP has expressed repeated support of the Third World, non-aligned news pool concept and has offered to make AP's experience available to young national agencies on a consultancy basis."[13] Reuters, UPI, and AFP have expressed a similar willingness to cooperate.

The Meaning of Imbalance

The accusation of imbalance is one of the criticisms most frequently leveled at the West in the media-flow debate. At its simplest level, as the *Washington Post* editorial acknowledges, the imbalance is most clearly seen in the anomaly that so many developing countries have foreigners handling their news for them, whether the flow is inward or outward.

As former Prime Minister Indira Gandhi commented at the New Delhi Ministerial Conference in July 1976: "We want to hear Africans on events in Africa. You should similarly be able to get an Indian explanation of events in India."

Sympathy toward this point of view is clearly not self-evident, however. Commenting directly on this statement, the International Press Institute said: "In our view it does not really matter what colour of skin you have, but whether or not you have the knowledge and integrity to do the job properly."[14]

Such a statement ignores the argument of those who insist that there can be differences in cultural viewpoint and perspective as well as skin color.

Another critic of Mrs. Gandhi's statement has been media sociologist Roger Tatarian, who commented: "Mrs.Gandhi's views would make Mr. Amin the judge of what the Indian public should know of Ugandan affairs."[15]

But it is clear that Mrs. Gandhi is not saying that *only* Africans should report on Africa, just that it happens too rarely. However, her argument can, with little difficulty, be extended: if there are few African journalists reporting on Africa for the Western media, the even greater anomaly is that there are so few Africans reporting to their compatriots from outside Africa. There are only four full-time journalists, all of them from South Africa, representing African papers in Washington, with the result that almost everything that Africans read or hear or see about the United States is written or spoken or photographed by non-Africans.

The extent of the domination of world news markets by major Anglo-American and French news services is well known. The two American-based agencies—Associated Press and United Press International—enjoy the lion's share, followed by Reuters and Agence France Press. The AP claims to have 10,000 members worldwide with about 1,300 newspaper members and 3,400 broadcasters in the U.S. and 110 member countries. It has been estimated that 1 billion people see or hear AP news each day. The UPI has 238 bureaus in 62 countries, employs a staff of more than 10,000, and has about 7,000 subscribers, including some 800 U.S. daily newspapers.

Reuters and AFP do not release complete figures of their operations on the ground that some of these could be misleading. However, it is known that Reuters has 17 regional circuits in 154 countries and puts out 1.5 million words a day in English, French, Spanish, Portuguese, Arabic, and German.

Nor can one discount the big newspaper news services, such as that of the *New York Times*, which is subscribed to by 136 or so foreign papers in 46 countries, and the *Los Angeles Times-Washington Post* service with 100 newspaper subscribers also in 46 countries.

A similar pattern exists in the supply of television news material. Visnews, the largest international supplier of news actuality material, has more than 170 clients and operates in almost every country where television exists, covering approximately 99 percent of all the television receivers in the world. Three quarters of Visnews is owned jointly by Reuters and the BBC, and the other quarter by public service organizations in Australia, Canada, and New Zealand. The second largest newsfilm agency, United Press Independent Television News (UPITN), is owned by UPI and by Independent Television News (ITN), London; UPI and Reuters provide UPITN and Visnews with an international communications network and a large supply of news. Visnews supplies BBC news film to NBC and also syndicates NBC material to the rest of the world. In turn, UPITN sells both ITN and UPI material overseas.

This means that the three major sellers of daily video news throughout the world are Anglo-American, with London and New York the twin capitals of a world news operation.

The advantage of these giant operations is economy of scale, whereby expensive news operations can be sold cheaply to many thousands of clients. The danger lies not so much in their potential for conspiracy as in the need to serve the requirements of the most profitable sectors of the market—which are to be found in the United States, Britain, the white Commonwealth, and Western Europe. It goes without saying that serving the needs of the most profitable market sectors can create an imbalance, not only with respect to ''peripheral'' countries but also in regions and ethnic groups within the Western market itself. For example, in a symposium of newsmen held at the University of California in 1967, Corky Trinidad of the *Philippines Herald* (Manila) discussed the use of the word Negro:

> We notice that stories on the wire frequently read ''John Smith, a negro, held up a bank''; ''Four negro youths attacked. . . .'' But we know that the United States population is made up of many groups, yet we don't see reports like ''Frank Sinatra , an Italian. . . .'' We cannot understand why there is always this emphasis on the word negro. And we notice that it is not used in the casualty lists from Vietnam. This type of identification helps to create an image of the negro as a savage, violent man. But there are many other savage, violent men. Oswald was not identified as a white man.

Discussing the sort of checkerboard censorship of Negro news in the U.S. southern press, Hodding Carter, editor of the Greenville, Mississippi, *Delta Democrat-Times*, says:

Not merely did it ignore what was occurring in the negro community, that is to say the really fundamental yearnings, changes, and tensions; it ran no news of the negro community whatsoever . . . except an incident of violence in which the negro could be seen as the perpetrator or the man at fault. We often enjoyed running the great stories of racial troubles elsewhere. I think that even today headlines in some deep South papers dwell heavily on each flare-up in New York or Los Angeles while ignoring as much as possible the march down the local main street. My point is that this was not a case of an evil conspiracy of bad men but of men totally reflecting the community in which they moved in the same way that most other newspaper publishers do. It was rather a natural thing.[16]

Another major element in the imbalance equation is the frequently publicized charge that the Western media rarely report on the Third World and that when they do they tend to concentrate largely on disasters, inefficiency, corruption, and tyranny. Exponents of this criticism have been at pains to point out that they are not asking so much for "pleasant" news as for a species of news that some have described as "developmental."

Narinder Aggarwala, an Indian journalist serving as regional information officer for Asia and the Pacific in the UN Development Program, puts it this way: "Developmental journalism is not so much different from what usually appears in Western newspapers in community or general news sections. But an international counterpart of community news is missing from Western media files."

This section of the debate is complicated by a multitude of arguments and a welter of confusing evidence. The initial reaction of the big news services is to claim that they do write generously—and accurately— about events in the Third World. Gerald Long said in November 1977: "We do in Reuters try very hard to give an accurate and rounded picture of events in a country—in other words, not to concentrate on the negative, on the criticism and the troubles." An Agence France Press statement similarly stressed its wide and sympathetic coverage of the Third World and shifted the blame on to its newspaper clients:

The distribution of news about the Third World countries is hindered by two major causes: either the lack of means or telecommunications or its excessive cost, or the limited or reserved welcome that the rest of the world gives to news from the Third World agencies . . . like most of the Western news agencies, *Agence France-Presse* has no power to impose on the French media, and even less so on foreign media, the use of news from the Third World agencies, no more than it can for its own reports from or about the Third World, even though this news is abundant, precise and interesting.[17]

This is emphatically an area in which there is a need for strictly empirical surveys. In a notable study, published late in 1973, on news agency reporting in Africa by Robert L. Bishop of the University of Michigan, it was demonstrated that Reuters and AFP showed little quantitative bias toward Britain and France. In stories about specific countries, Reuters mentioned Britain only 3 percent of the time on its English wires and 9 percent on its French wires. AFP mentioned France only 6 percent of the time. On the other hand, both of them mentioned African countries in about 40 percent of such cases.[18]

The Bishop study suggests that there should be a closer look at the criticisms about "disaster" reporting since such stories accounted for only 2 percent of the stories for Reuters and AFP. But stories from Africa on economic, educational, cultural, medical, and scientific topics ranged from 23 percent to 33 percent on the test output.

The problem is that, despite their appearance on the wire services, important developmental themes often are ignored in parts of the Third World itself. A statistical survey conducted in Latin American papers in November 1975 showed that Third World news tends to go unnoticed in Latin American newspapers.

Newspapers throughout Latin America were studied over a four-day period to see how well an important item of Third World news was picked up. The story, originating in Geneva and released by AP, AFP, and Prensa Latina (Cuba), told of a UN report claiming that thousands of pharmaceutical products were being foisted unnecessarily on Third World countries. Except in Mexico, the story went almost unnoticed. The survey showed that there were many other cases of this kind, and the author's conclusion was that "development" themes are not "news" and therefore not interesting in Latin America. Its author blamed "external news domination" and "colonial stereotypes" for this state of affairs.

> Professional shortcomings and distortions persist in this area of journalism more than in others . . . in all but a few papers there is no capacity for an independent interpretation of world or regional affairs. Few newspapers have correspondents of their own in key capitals or send reporters to cover important events. . . . There is subjection to dominant models in the overemphasis of events of little or no importance to Latin America.[19]

What are these dominant models, and can we shed some critical light on their formation?

What Is "News"?

A hundred years ago, AP's first leased wire was capable of transmitting 20,000 words a day from New York to Washington. Today, computers and satellites are part of the everyday language of newspaper communications in the West, and AP can boast that it has made computer-to-computer transmissions at speeds of approximately 56,000 words per minute. And yet despite this extraordinary revolution in communications, there seems to have been no corresponding increase in foreign coverage in Western newspapers.

In fact, U.S. as well as British newspapers have been reducing the amount of foreign news they use. A recent survey of fifty-four U.S. newspaper editors by AP managing editors showed that, although the majority of them believed that foreign news was important, they felt that they were printing too much of it. Nearly half the editors reported that they were therefore cutting back on their international coverage and for the most part not assigning a specific amount of space to foreign news.

At the same time, there is some evidence that the corps of adequately trained correspondents abroad is dwindling. Surveys have demonstrated that the number of full-time U.S. foreign correspondents was 676 in 1975—down 28 percent from 929 in 1969. Europe continued to dominate U.S. overseas coverage, with 51 percent of all American correspondents headquartered there. Asia was second to Europe in 1975, with 23 percent, or 160 U.S. correspondents. Two out of every three U.S. correspondents in Asia were in Southeast Asia, mainly in Hong Kong; one-third were in East Asia, mainly in Japan.[20]

It is commonly argued that economic factors are behind the shrinking foreign "news holes," as some editors call them. But does this mean that it has become prohibitively expensive for papers to gather foreign news that they desperately want? Or is it, rather, the result of news values that, by and large, are the consequence of editors' notions as to what their readers want—in other words, what will sell papers (a different kind of economic argument)?

News values that are heavily based on the consensus requirements of readers cannot be condemned out of hand, but it must be asked how they measure up to Roger Tatarian's "litmus test" quoted by Leonard R. Sussman: "There are two broad currents in the global stream of information. One is news, the other propaganda. They are more easily defined by purpose than content. The purpose of news is simply to inform. The purpose of propaganda is to influence."[21]

Professor B. C. Cohen, in *The Press and American Foreign Policy*, found that on the average American newspapers print only about one-sixth of the material coming in to them from the AP alone. Even a paper like the *New York Times*, which averages 90 pages during the week and 600 on Sunday, is able to print only about 15 percent of the material that reaches its editors' desks.

The power of editors over what constitutes "news" is therefore considerable; so is the editors' freedom to slant the news and dress it up to capture readers' attention. "I remember very clearly a speech I gave in Nashville," recalled Mayor Charles Evers of Fayette, Mississippi. "I said: 'If the whites don't stop beating and mistreating and burning our churches and killing our brothers and sisters, we're going to shoot back.' What did the headline say the next day? EVERS SAYS NEGROES WILL SHOOT WHITES. This kind of thing goes on all the time."[22]

In a survey conducted by Professor B. Key in the late 1960s, 47 percent of a sample of the adult population in the United States admitted that they read "just the headlines."

But the "choice" of foreign news in Western papers is not just a question of selection from raw copy. It often is a positive process whereby an editor anticipates a story, assigns it, and describes how he wants it written. He "sees" a story of a particular event and shapes it ahead of time according to a set of preconceived notions. A typical example of this is the coronation of "Emperor" Bokassa in Bangui, which probably received more coverage in two weeks than a major African country, such as Zambia, receives in a decade.

Nobody will deny that the story was bizarre, extravagant, and amusing—and therefore very readable. It also was an expensive story to cover, and there was a great deal of competition for the best pictures and anecdotes. The Bangui story, however, was typical of the sort of event that makes news around the Third World, and it was told *against* the Third World—the pathetic "black savage" dressed in emperor's clothes, aping the behavior of former colonial masters.

Were editors prepared to spend as much on sending journalists to the UNCTAD talks last summer?

The Bangui story was clearly affected by the value system of the commercial market for news features, whereby stories are bought and sold like so many bales of cloth. Feature salesmen talk of articles as being "premium category"; they are constantly searching for "blockbusters" and "big-name" writers. "Exclusives" are auctioned off throughout the world as "properties." In this sense, the world of "news" merges with the world of entertainment. And the purchasing price of a news feature often affects both the play it gets in the paper and the degree to which it is promoted.

Against this background, editors—and readers—might rate the doings of Margaret Trudeau or Jacqueline Onassis as being of greater significance than those of an important statesman. Countries can be categorized as being sources of particular types of color stories—soap opera'' in Italy, ''the Royal Family'' in Britain, ''escaped Nazi war criminals'' in Latin America, Amin's ''buffoonery'' in Uganda, and so forth.

On the other hand, Western news values also are affected by the tendency toward crisis stories. Such stories get prominence and good play, and journalists and editors are tempted to reject other kinds of news in their favor or to add a taste of crisis to stories that do not really merit such treatment.

The Guardian's Martin Woollacott reports that ''in the Philippines few Western reporters visit model land reform projects in Luzon; but hundreds have gone down to Mindanao to cover the war between Muslim secessionists and the Government party. . . .'' A Filipino information official told Woollacott: ''It is as if Western reporters feel their job in any developing society is to identify that society's weakest points and biggest problems and then make them worse by exaggeration and unremitting publicity.'' Woollacott comments that perhaps the crisis in reporting results from the ''West's deep disillusion with nearly all post-colonial societies, as well as the Western assumption that the West is still the ultimate arbiter of the rest of the world.''[23]

Crisis orientation in Western journalism applies as much to treatment as it does to theme. As one *New York Times* journalist describes it: ''News reporting, which is so wedded to the sudden, the jerk, the sharp break in continuity, finds it difficult to report the incremental, the casual, the imperceptible shifts in the affairs of man that cumulatively more often than not shape life on our planet.''[24]

And as Paul Hoch comments: ''When we read 'news' of an assassination, a revolution, an election, or whatever we are seldom encouraged . . . to ask why this or that happened, how the situation developed, how the 'event' in question was related to its socio-economic environment, or how things might have been different.''

The temptation to ''play up'' a story can lead not only to undue sensationalism but also to deliberate distortion and inaccuracy. Journalists often have blamed editorial pressure and the competitive values of Western journalism for this.

Every foreign correspondent has his memory of a bogus story. David Ottaway of the *Washington Post* gives this account of reporting the war in Ethiopia:

> We have the news agency reports in bitter, 24-hour competition to beat each other onto the world's front pages and often feeling themselves obliged to turn believable rumors into hard war reports in order to keep editors back home happy, and hopefully to win the morning or night cycle of news on Ethiopia. Under the best of conditions, news agency reporting is a tough, extremely competitive sport in which the writer with a sharp dramatic war

lead is certain to win hands down over his more cautious colleagues . . . an American news agency, on a quiet weekend, reported soldiers and civilians engaged for an hour in "street fighting" on the very outskirts of Addis Ababa. But all that other journalists could verify was a handful of shots fired when police attempted to arrest a single Eritrean. The agency, however, had added authority to its report by quoting "diplomatic sources"—and what editor, or indeed reader, could then doubt its authenticity: . . . It's easy to criticize this kind of journalism but all too easy to become swept up in the game under the pressure to give editors and readers some version at least of developments in the war.[25]

The very scarcity of available space increases the tendency to exaggerate a story and provides a constant goad to reporters to portray their stories in the most dramatic light.

Meanwhile, there are similar temptations for the rewrite man, as mentioned by John Gordon, editor of the *Sunday Express*, when he appeared before the 1949 Royal Commission on the press: "Striving to squeeze something extra out of a story, [he] will disregard the reporter's facts and substitute what he imagines to be better 'facts.'"

These criticisms of the Western press as being "crisis oriented" and prone to slanting news and headlines are not exclusive to controversies with the Third World; they are heard as frequently in discussions about the press within Western society itself. There are, however, greater sensitivities on the part of the Third World that perhaps are not entirely unjustified: for their societies—and, indeed, for Western relations with them—a great deal is at stake in balancing both their difficulties and their achievements.

Language and Cultural Imperialism

The UPI filed the following dispatch from its New York office on February 27, 1974:

A MEETING OF A NUMBER OF THE MAIN BAUXITE-PRODUCING COUNTRIES SCHEDULED TENTATIVELY FOR MARCH 5 IN CONAKRY (GUINEA) HAS CAUSED UNDERSTANDABLE CONCERN IN WASHINGTON. SOME EXPERTS FEEL THAT THE CONFERENCE COULD BE THE FIRST STEP IN THE ESTABLISHMENT OF A SERIES OF INTERNATIONAL CARTELS FOR CONTROLLING RAW MATERIALS ESSENTIAL TO THE INDUSTRIAL NATIONS WHICH COULD SET THE UNITED STATES' ECONOMY BACK MORE THAN 40 YEARS.

The cable was taken up by sociologist Juan Somavia and cited in a paper given at the Mexico Seminar on Information in 1976. Somavia

charged that it was "news" of this kind that created the impression in
industrialized countries that the increasing capacity of the raw material-
producing countries to organize themselves better in defense of their
interests was a "threat" to their own development. Somavia went on:

> It is inferred that it is "legitimate" for the industrialised countries to
> defend themselves and to seek by all means at their disposal to obstruct the
> organisational capacity of the Third World. At the same time, the cable
> warns the countries meeting in Conakry that Washington's concern is
> "understandable" and that, consequently, if they should come to an agree-
> ment on bauxite, it would be logical that reprisals might be forthcoming.[26]

In this particular instance, the point of view of the writer is very clear,
but so is that of his intended readership. But critics of the Western
agencies stress that there is a consistent display of prejudice in a less
obvious way—through their consistent use of biased language even in
seemingly neutral copy.

In his book, *The Great Fear in Latin America*, John Gerassi claimed
that in Latin America AP and UPI were regarded by the politically astute
as U.S. government agencies because of their use of language:

> And it is not hard to see why: their dispatches turn every politician that
> criticises the United States into a "leftist," most peasant leaders that
> demand a better living standard into "demagogues," and all Castro sup-
> porters into "Communists."
>
> When Brazil's President Joao Goulart appointed Francisco Brochado da
> Rocha as premier, the *New York Times* reported that "Dr. Brochado Rocha
> is a member of the conservative Social Democratic Party." . . . But the
> premier, conservative as he was, insisted that under his direction, Brazil
> would maintain a hands-off Cuba policy; that, presumably, made him
> anti-United States. Later the *New York Times* said: "Premier Brochado da
> Rocha is a member of the middle-of-the-road Social Democratic Party."
> Then on the very next day a *Times* editorial referred to the premier as a
> "leftist."

One does not have to take a strongly leftist stance to recognize that the
Western media take a north-to-south view of the world as well as a
west-to-east one. Those capable of a detached view should therefore
appreciate that what was to the United States an "incursion" into
Cambodia was to the Cambodians an "invasion." Similarly, a "Negro
problem" for white Americans might be a "white racist" problem for
black Americans.

At the same time, we are aware that "terrorist" (rather than "guerrilla"), "guns" (rather than "weapons"), and a hundred other heavily
loaded stereotypes are an important part of the shorthand of journalism

and inevitably cause some to feel that they have been made the victims of bias.

The problems raised by language in the flow of information are numerous. They have to do with the cultural and political orientation of both the writer and the service he works for and also with the need to write briefly and simply about complex issues that sometimes involve entire continents.

The extent to which agencies offend the Third World in their use of pejorative language is difficult to assess, and any criticism should be backed by a painstaking survey. For their part, agencies are conscious of the problem. For example, Reuters has a standing rule that the word "terrorist" should never be used. This does not mean, of course, that papers do not alter agency copy to suit their viewpoint.

One correspondent from the Middle East, Joseph Fitchett, complained to *The Observer*'s Foreign News Service that the *Jerusalem Post* as a matter of course changed the term "guerrilla" in his copy to "terrorist" whenever it applied to Arabs. On the other hand, in his study, *The Press in Developing Countries*, E. Lloyd Sommerlad says that the subeditors on African papers got so used to changing "terrorists" to "freedom fighters" on the agency files that it became a reflex action.

Practicing journalists are only too conscious of their ability, and their editors' ability, to adopt stereotyped language in order to make copy crisper and more economical, particularly in "capsule" reports. Terms such as "Peking-oriented," "banana republic," "military-style government," "strife-torn," and "sleeping giant" are useful in the short, pithy report, but such labels also can be superficial, glib, and insulting—not to say misleading for Western readers.

At the same time, there is a tendency to use stereotypes euphemistically when applying them to the West. As Paul Hoch notes:

> To bomb more hell out of a tiny Asian country in one year than was bombed out of Europe in the whole Second World War becomes "escalation." Threatening to burn and blast to death several million civilians in an enemy country is called "deterrence." Turning a city into a radioactive rubble is called "taking out" a city. A concentration camp (already a euphemism for a political prison) becomes a "strategic hamlet." A comparison of the slaughter on both sides in a war is called a "kill ratio." Totalling up the corpses is called a "body count." Running the blacks out of town is called "urban renewal" . . . .[27]

From Hoch's Marxist standpoint, this use of language proves that there is a conspiracy to falsify and propagandize, but it is possible to criticize this type of journalism without being a Marxist or subscribing to conspiracy theories. Western ethnocentricity has a long history, but Westerners are not alone in adopting toward the rest of the world strongly ethnocentric views—and language molded to these views.

In his essay "Reporting from the Third World," Mort Rosenblum described the sort of situation that makes for flawed and even distorted reports: "Correspondents frequently cannot speak the language of the country they are covering, and translators, if available, are rarely adequate. Unfamiliarity with baffling local customs and thought processes can be dangerously misleading. Under such circumstances, even the best have difficulty, and some reporters working abroad are simply not capable of untangling complicated situations and presenting them clearly to far-away readers."

Against this background, the dominant role of the English language through the big Western agencies is a matter of concern to many Third World countries. At the 1976 Mexico Seminar on Information, Fred da Silva, former editor of the *Ceylon Daily News*, cited Sri Lanka as typical of those countries where colonial dependence had been perpetuated by the dominant role of English despite the fact that not even 5 percent of the country (whose population is now approaching 14 million) could be identified as English-educated or -speaking:

> Sri Lanka's Press Trust is among 90 national agencies which are ill-disguised branch offices linked in a subservient and colonial relationship to their dominant partner in the former imperial headquarters. Reuters of London still dictates the shape, substance and stress bestowed on every item of news flowing both inwards and outwards from Sri Lanka. Many studies could be devoted to examining the daily distortions of the information and comment that is supplied to our readers about events in the world for over half a century.

Critics such as da Silva point out that the domination of English and French is part of the north-to-south physical communications systems and that what is missing from the information flows of the world is an adequate and direct "lateral" flow among developing countries. Can there be any doubt that regional news agencies based in South America, Asia, and Africa would help answer the needs and aspirations of many of the countries that feel an important dimension of information is missing in their societies? The Asian viewpoint has been eloquently expressed by Kuldip Nayar, former chief of United News of India, in a paper prepared for the Press Institute of India:

> We Asians form almost two-thirds of the world's population, and I am sure we should make news by the dint of numbers alone. . . . We have a point of view which needs to be expressed fully and adequately. You may

call it the Eastern point of view or the Asian. . . . It is a point of view with a positive content—something different, something real. We who have been subject people for centuries, we who have always looked towards Washington, London or Paris are not free to fend for ourselves. We have a history, we have a culture, a tradition. We are not just a jumble of events, names and dates thrown about, as the West generally depicts us and probably sees us. We represent a whole stream of thought, a wave of reaction, traditions reaching far into the past, a distinct attitude and a way of life.No doubt, we are affected by European problems, but emotionally we are stirred by our own Asian and African problems. . . . The reawakening in Asia is a fascinating theme, and we are now conscious participants in each country, in this undertaking. Why not report on what we hope to achieve, when we are going to achieve it and how far we have progressed? Today what the world news agencies generally pick up and disseminate in Asia and elsewhere is a story of some riot or of hungry and famished Asians. These are correct stories but there are so many other things happening. I admit there are laudable exceptions. Seldom do Western news agencies report the progress we have made towards development. It is the same as news coming from Latin America always relating to revolution, military coup d'etats or earthquakes. . . . I analysed the news put across in a week by three different news agencies bought by my agency. The total foreign news items issued during the week were 923: out of this, 15 percent were from Asia. There was not a single day when the stories originating from Asia went beyond 20, compared to an average of more than 110 from the West.

The Impact of Radio on Information Flows

Lenin once described radio as a newspaper without paper. Its potential for reaching large audiences, for crossing the boundaries of illiteracy as well as of politics and territory, make it a particularly powerful means of communication in the Third World.

Another feature is its immediacy and speed—enabling its controllers to inform audiences and to comment on events as they are happening. Nobody can doubt the special power of radio to influence human beings in a profound way. Perhaps the most famous instance in the Western world is the Orson Welles science-fiction broadcast in America in 1938 that caused hundreds of thousands of people to flee their homes. And those who listened to the BBC during World War II remember the extraordinary power of radio in lifting civilian morale.

In many Third World countries, the power of radio is intensified by the importance of verbal tradition. In Africa, it is known as the ''Palaver tradition,'' the recounting of legends and myths, folk tales, proverbs, and riddles. Moreover, it is easy to understand how in countries where there are many languages or dialects, and poor transportation, broadcasting has a distinct advantage.

According to UNESCO's 1971 *Statistical Handbook*, there were 45 radio receivers—and only 11 newspapers—to every 1,000 Africans. According to a 1972 survey in Zambia, 77 percent of the population learned of news events only through radio broadcasting. In *Muffled Drums*, William Hachten provides these statistics as of 1971 for Africa as a whole, excluding Egypt: only about 175 newspapers circulated about 2.7 million copies daily, some 98 radio stations broadcast to 12.5 million radio receivers, 32 television stations transmitted to roughly 428,000 receiving sets, about 525 weeklies and fortnightlies had a combined circulation of more than 3.8 million, about 5,000 indoor motion picture theaters had about 1.3 million seats, and some 3,800 local libraries contained almost 14.8 million books.

The north-to-south flow of international communications is an extension and development of the one-way traffic from Europe to outposts of empire. Radio services were originally established to keep the settlers in touch with the home country, and only gradually did the indigenous (that is, the more Europeanized) population join the audience. On becoming independent, the new nations in Africa, for example, did not inherit radio systems suitable for assistance in nation-building: neither did they inherit indigenous personnel, funds, or equipment. Many still are relying on Europeans for their technical expertise in radio.

External broadcasts into the Third World from the industrialized world, both West and East, have been one of the most important factors in information flow during this century. The United States, the Soviet Union, China, and the Warsaw Pact countries are building more stations and increasing their output in power, program hours, and number of languages. Poland has recently erected a transmitter of 2 megawatts (2 million watts), and Yugoslavia is constructing two 1-megawatt transmitters that, when used with directional aerials, will be the world's most powerful. The BBC, for many years considered to be at the forefront of external broadcasting, uses transmitters from 250,000 to 500,000 watts.

Voice of America has huge relay complexes staked out in many parts of the Third World itself—for example, its station at Monrovia, Liberia, where its massive wattage can be even more effectively deployed from African soil.

The revolution in transistor production has brought about a huge increase in radio ownership in developing countries, in some cases doubling within the last seven years. In 1970, there were about 13.5 million radio sets in India; by 1977, the estimate had risen to 25 million. In the Middle East, the number went from 17.2 million to 30 million over the same period; in Latin America, from 43.3 million to about 77 million.[28]

The extent to which states have recognized the power of radio is amply demonstrated by the length to which some have gone to prevent people from listening to ''outside'' broadcasts. In Nazi-occupied Europe, death sentences could be handed down for those found listening to the BBC, and during the Algerian war for independence, the French banned the sale of radio sets. In addition to imposing penalties, some countries, notably Russia, have spent huge sums of money on jamming. In Nazi Germany, a solution to foreign listening was the sale of the two-valve ''People's Set,'' which was too weak to receive outside signals.

E. T. Lean wrote in *Voices in the Darkness* (1943) that in the case of Nazi Germany, ''the effect of those elaborate precautions was to stimulate curiosity of those who had been afraid to listen and to convert them into regular listeners.''

The United States, the Soviet Union, Great Britain, Germany, and China are at the forefront of an expensive exercise to expand their audiences and pump information into the Third World.

The United States and the Soviet Union broadcast more than 2,000 program hours each week in many languages to audiences throughout Third World countries. China, the world's third largest broadcaster, puts out 1,400 program hours a week, and Great Britain and Germany broadcast more than 700 hours each.

Over the past twenty years, there has been something of a battle for domination of the wave bands—particularly into Africa. Soviet broadcasting to Africa began in April 1958 with a fifteen-minute program in English and French. In 1960 came the first Swahili broadcast; by then, the Soviet Union was broadcasting 33.5 hours a week to Africa. Broadcasting was stepped up to 120 hours by 1964, and the languages now include Hausa, Lingala, Malagasy, Somali, Zulu, and Bambara, as well as English, French, and Italian.

By 1966, Soviet broadcasting time exceeded 120 hours a week, compared with the BBC's 57 hours (in 5 languages only), despite the fact that Great Britain had firm, traditional links with a large part of Africa. In 1975, Soviet broadcasting to Africa had reached 167 hours a week in 14 languages.[29]

There is considerable controversy among students as to the role and effect of international broadcasting. Some important questions remain unanswered: How many people listen? How much are they influenced? To what extent are foreign states aided in their policy by the use of international broadcasting?

Answers to these questions should shed light on the central paradox of foreign broadcasting: while it is clearly an outstanding means for the free flow of information, it also is one of the most powerful means in developing countries for the dissemination of propaganda.

The major international broadcasters employ various techniques to estimate the size of their audiences—instituting "listener's panels" and sample surveys of various kinds. Figures often are held to be unreliable, however, as external services have budgets to justify, not to mention the vested interest they have in producing the most favorable figures.[30]

Both the United States and the Soviet Union have developed their major external services—Voice of America and Radio Moscow—from government information agencies. Voice of America is the official voice of the U.S. government; it is state funded, and has its policy laid down by directives from the U.S. Information Agency. Since 1953, its goal has been "to submit evidence to the peoples of other nations by means of communication techniques that the objectives and policies of the US are in harmony with and advance their legitimate aspirations for freedom, peace and progress."[31]

The goals of Moscow's external radio policy are to "skillfully consider the particular features of individual countries and sections of the population and provide broad coverage of the life and foreign and domestic policies of the Soviet Union; publicize the achievements of the world system of socialism; comprehensively illustrate the international importance of the USSR's experience of Communist construction," and "reveal the anti-popular politics of the imperialist states. . . ."[32]

Ironically, Radio Moscow's main propaganda thrust against the United States is to counter Voice of America's frequent reference nowadays to the free information principles inherent in "Basket III" of the Helsinki conference. Moscow argues, in fact, that the American policy of the "free flow of information"—as evidenced by Voice of America itself—constitutes interference in the internal affairs of the Soviet Union and "other sovereign states."[33]

The other large international service, the External Services of the BBC, is financed by a Parliamentary grant-in-aid, the cost of which is borne by the Foreign and Commonwealth Office. The BBC enjoys independence from government control, and has avoided two major attempts to subject it to government censorship: during World War II and during the Suez crisis.

Despite its high standards of balanced reporting and views, the External Services nevertheless plays an important role in projecting Great Britain's image as a major industrial power abroad.

Operating on a severely restricted budget, it has faced numerous cuts in recent years; significantly, one of the more serious cuts involved the discontinuation of broadcasts in indigenous languages to developing countries.

Any discussion of news flow must clearly take into account both the effect and growth of broadcasting and the extent to which it is a one-way flow, heavily slanted toward the interests of its government sponsors.

As we have seen, the number of receivers in the Third World has dramatically increased in recent years. But has there been any corresponding output of broadcasting from south to north? And to what extent has there been an increase in "lateral" flow? These are the questions that remain to be answered.

Notes

Chapter I

1. The main resolutions on improving the flow of information adopted at the Algiers meeting were:

a. Reorganize existing communications channels, which are a legacy of the colonial past and which hamper free, direct, and fast communication.

b. Seek to revise existing multilateral agreements in order to review press cable rates and to initiate faster and cheaper intercommunication.

c. Take urgent steps to expedite the process of collective ownership of communications satellites and to evolve a code of conduct for directing their use.

d. Promote contact among the mass media, universities, libraries, planning and research bodies, and other institutions in order to enable developing countries to share expertise, ideas, and experience.

The provision calling for the "collective ownership of communications satellites" and for a "code of conduct" set the stage for the subsequent controversy over direct satellite television broadcasts and the enormously complex question of "prior consent" on the part of those countries to whom these transmissions were to be beamed.

2. Rosemary Righter, *Whose News?* (London: Burnett Books, 1978).

Chapter II

1. Quoted in paper read to the Twenty-sixth General Assembly of the International Press Institute, entitled "Cultural Imperialism and the Media," p. 4.

2. Paper presented at the conference on "The Third World and Press Freedom" sponsored by the Edward R. Murrow Center of the Fletcher School of Law and Diplomacy, Tufts University.

3. Quoted by Shashi Tharoor, "Information Imbalances," *Fletcher Forum* I (Spring 1977).

4. Juan Somavia, *The Transnational Power Structure and International Information* (Mexico City: ILET, 1976), p. 8.

5. Dilip Mukerjee, "Kya Samachar?" *Illustrated Weekly of India,* October 10, 1976, pp. 10–11.

6. *Freedom at Issue,* No. 37 (September–October 1976), p.4.

7. Richard Hoggart, "The Mass Media: A New Colonialism?" The Eighth STC Communication Lecture, London, 1978.

8. Quoted by Tharoor, "Information Imbalances," p. 29.

9. Ibid.

10. Hilary Ng'weno, *The Weekly Review* (Nairobi), November 8, 1977.

11. Leonard R. Sussman, *Mass News Media and the Third World Challenge,* The Washington Papers. Vol. V. The Center for Strategic and International Studies, Georgetown University, Washington, D.C. (Beverly Hills/London: Sage Publications, 1977).

12. Peter Galliner, *Access to Information—an International Problem* (London: International Press Institute).

13. Edward T. Pinch, *The Third World and the Fourth Estate: A Look at the Non-aligned News Agency Pool.* Senior Seminar in Foreign Policy.U.S. Department of State, Washington, D.C. (1976/77).

14. Mort Rosenblum, "Reporting from the Third World," *Foreign Affairs* (July 1977).

15. Ng'weno, *The Weekly Review*.

16. Hoggart, "The Mass Media."

Chapter III

1. "Access to Information," International Press Institute paper (1977), p. 7.

2. George Orwell, *Collected Essays*, Vol. IV (London: Penguin Books, 1970), pp. 81–82.

3. *International Herald Tribune (IHT)*, Paris, January 3, 1977, p. 7.

4. Jeremy Tunstall, *The Media Are American* (New York: Columbia University Press, 1977), pp.38–39.

5. Paul Hoch, *The Newspaper Game*, (London: Calder & Boyars, Ltd., 1974).

6. *Daily Telegraph* (London), July 28, 1976.

7. UNESCO Aide-Memoire DADG/CC/COM/48/ Paris, July 30, 1976.

8. "Access to Information," p. 2.

9. Monograph on AP prepared for UNESCO, 1973, pp. 13–15.

10. *IHT*, January 6, 1978, p. 3.

11. *Washington Post*, April 22, 1977, p. C4.

12. *IPI Report*, November 1976, p. 9

13. AP Monograph, p. 13.

14. "Access to Information," p. 4.

15. Paper on news flow commissioned by the Edward R. Murrow Center, March 1978, p. 13.

16. Quoted in Hoch, *The Newspaper Game*, pp. 128–129.

17. Agence France Press statement on Third World news pool (1977), p. 7.

18. "Third World and the Fourth Estate," U.S. Department of State, seminar 1976–1977, p. 5

19. *Development Dialogue*, 1976, 2, p. 41.

20. Ralph Kliesch "The Press Corps Abroad Revisited." Quoted in *Journal of Communications* (Winter 1976), p.49.

21. Sussman, *Mass News Media*.

22. Quoted in Hoch, *The Newspaper Game*, p. 93.

23. "In Search of Bad News," *New Straits Times*, September 2, 1975, p. 10.

24. Jonathan Power, "Still New Under the Sun: Truth," *New York Times*, November 7, 1975. Quoted in *Journal of Communications* (Winter 1977).

25. *Washington Post*, February 26, 1975.

26. *Development Dialogue*, 1976, 2, p. 21.

27. Hoch, *The Newspaper Game*, p. 133.

28. Figures from *World Radio and Television Receivers* (London: BBC, 1977).

29. James O. H. Nason, "International Broadcasting as an Instrument of Foreign Policy," *Journal of International Studies*, Vol. VI, p. 128.

30. Julian Hale, *Radio Power: Propaganda on International Broadcasting* (Philadelphia: Temple University Press, 1975), passim; Ian Greig, *The Communist Challenge to Africa* (Richmond, Great Britain: Foreign Affairs Publishing Co., Ltd., 1977), pp. 97–99.

31. T. H. Qualter, *Propaganda and Psychological Warfare* (Philadelphia: Philadelphia Book Co., Inc., 1962), p.122.

32. Hale, *Radio Power*, p. 18.

33. Nason, ''International Broadcasting,'' p. 141.